FROM TINKERING TO TRANSFORMATION

FROM TINKERING TO TRANSFORMATION

*How School District Central Offices Drive
Equitable Teaching and Learning*

Meredith I. Honig and Lydia R. Rainey

Harvard Education Press
Cambridge, Massachusetts

Paperback ISBN 978-1-68253-843-2

Library of Congress Cataloging-in-Publication Data is on file.

Published by Harvard Education Press,
an imprint of the Harvard Education Publishing Group

Harvard Education Press
8 Story Street
Cambridge, MA 02138

Cover Design: Wilcox Design
Cover Image: Yang Zhuo/Moment via Getty Images

The typefaces in this book are Sabon and Futura.

Contents

Acknowledgments

We were talking with a cabinet-level leader from a large suburban district after she and her team finished running a multiday professional learning session on equity and antiracism for about forty senior central office leaders, including deputies, chiefs, associates, and principal supervisors. The session was state of the art, challenging participants to identify how they, in their central office roles, could advance equitable teaching and learning using case studies, simulations, reviews of research, and other modalities and materials that helped participants confront their positionality and the district's role in perpetuating racism. Staff feedback on the session was overwhelmingly positive, with all participants agreeing or strongly agreeing that the session pushed their thinking and that they would be better agents of equity as a result.

But the cabinet-level leader was deflated. The activities throughout the five days emphasized that school systems have historically not advanced equity and that doing better would require fundamentally different ways of working across the central office. The culminating activity asked participants what specific shifts in their work they would now make, but their ideas mainly reflected modest adjustments in their personal behavior. For example, some said that they would approach their interactions with colleagues with more sensitivity to the historical marginalization of students and staff members of color. Others said that they would use some of the activities from the session in meetings with their own staff. Many wanted to learn more. But the cabinet-level leader didn't hear any examples of fundamental shifts participants planned to make in their core work, such as new approaches to teacher professional development, school improvement planning, or recruitment and hiring.

She asked, "What did we miss?"

We reviewed the design and execution of the learning session together and agreed it was, in fact, state of the art in terms of materials and methods related to educational equity. But the field has been missing a key resource—reliable ideas about *the kinds of fundamental systemic shifts in central offices* that advance equitable teaching and learning. Most of the materials her staff members had found to use in the session came from school-level—not central-office-level— experiences and research. All the materials focused on changes in individual mind-sets and dispositions, and some called for new policy goals like increasing the number of students of color who access advanced coursework. Her staff also touched on the growing body of work that emphasizes community engagement and leadership for advancing equity. But none of the materials prompted staff members to reimagine their work more fundamentally with equity at the core. She reflected, "We even said that racism and inequities operate on multiple levels: individual, interpersonal, organizational, and institutional. But we left off that whole last piece. . . . Where's the content for that?"

For almost two decades, we have had the good fortune to study and partner with school district central office leaders across the country as they grappled with institutional-level change in service of equitable teaching and learning. They knew that their work was going to take, in the words of one superintendent, "nothing less than a total district transformation" of the assumptions and values that had historically driven their central office. And to varying degrees, they achieved institutional shifts across their central office.

In this book, we share what we learned together about how central offices can drive equitable teaching and learning. We hope the findings and examples throughout this book begin to address gaps in content in educational equity work. We also hope they provide some welcome guidance and inspiration to central office leaders and staff members, so many of whom aim to advance educational equity every day but often find themselves stuck in deeply entrenched central office systems working in other directions without reliable guides for how to get unstuck. And as we express in the conclusion, we offer the ideas in this book as a floor, not a ceiling—a new foundation for rethinking central offices that we hope leaders will use as a starting point to help them discover what's next.

Any project that is almost two decades in the making benefits from many collaborators and supporters along the way, and this one is no exception. We are forever grateful to Mike Knapp for securing the funding and flexibility for our first study of central office transformation, especially at a time when interest and faith in central offices among policy makers and funders was at a definite low. Without those resources and his encouragement, we likely would not have been able to initiate or advance this research program. Mike Copland was the co-Principal Investigator on our first central office transformation study and collaborated on conceptualizing the second, always keeping the focus on generating knowledge that matters for leaders' practice.

Our research assistants made various essential contributions to this work over the years, including asking great questions, ensuring that we captured detailed data, and helping make our projects fun. Special thanks go to Aly Honsa, Juli Lawton, Patricia McNeil, Morena Newton, Jenee Myers Twitchell, Nitya Venkateswaran, and Emily Donaldson Walsh.

Our funders supported our time and effort on the various projects that contributed to this book and were also invaluable thought partners and cheerleaders. Thank you to the Wallace Foundation, the William T. Grant Foundation, and the Spencer Foundation. We are especially grateful for the sage advice and encouragement we received from Rochelle Herring and Kim DuMont.

Our main goal in all our work is to find leaders who are taking promising and unavoidably challenging ideas about advancing educational equity and trying to put them into action—to learn with and from them over time and, in the process, elevate and share their experiences that might otherwise go unseen. Our ability to do any of that depends on the willingness of those leaders to open up their practice, share their rough-draft thinking, and trust us to represent their words and their work. Those leaders include people in our research sites as well as our partner districts who invited us to help them use our initial findings to advance central office transformation in their districts and learn with them along the way. Our confidentiality agreements prevent us from naming them. We hope they recognize their influence and inspiration on the following pages.

We dedicate this book to each and every one of them.

It Takes a System

PRINCIPAL MONICA TORRES thought her time had finally come.[1] The new district superintendent had a powerful vision for educational equity and promised sweeping reform of the central office. "He's the first to come along and really talk about how the central office needs to be a support and partner to schools. And that we need to root out racism and other inequities throughout the district—not just in schools but in the central office too." Principal Torres knew well the importance of that vision. She identified as Latina, and as a student, she was routinely pulled out of her classes to receive special services for students with limited English proficiency and economic disadvantage. She reflected, "To get help with what's happening in the classroom, you got pulled out of the classroom. I had to work twice as hard not to let all that help leave me further behind—behind the White kids."

She went into education to tackle those inequities and encountered others. In her first interview for a teaching position, the recruiter kept pronouncing her name wrong and seemed especially critical of her credentials, probing her readiness to teach science and math and her interest in a language specialist position instead. Once in the classroom, she had to supplement the district curriculum materials and approaches to reflect the diversity of her students. She spent far more time as an assistant principal than her White peers despite her stellar performance reviews. And once a principal, she was inundated with operational and compliance matters. She explained, "I've had to be my own kind of equity warrior. I protect my own time. I build relationships with the right people in the central office so I can get things done. But that's its own kind of inequity—that I can get the services I need because of who I know."

Two years after the arrival of the new superintendent, she's still waiting. According to Principal Torres, "The superintendent is always talking about this big transformation. But what is it? I see that the Curriculum and Instruction office is now called Learning, Leading, and Innovation. Some positions got cut. We've got new people at the top, including an equity officer, which is a nice idea, but what can one person do? I've had more visits from central office staff because their new mandate is to hear more from principals. I know they love the visits. For me, they take my time, my teachers get a little stressed, and in the end, it's all the same."

PRINCIPAL JASON JONES also had a new superintendent who came in with a strong equity vision that included "tackling the systemic roots of inequities across the central office." That systemic approach resonated strongly with him. In high school, he had been one of a handful of African American students in honors classes. He became a teacher to encourage more students like him. But by the time many of those students reached his high school history classes, they were so far behind in other subjects that there was only so much he could do. He pursued his current principalship at an alternative high school, in his words, "to get away from the central office. Here, we are free from a lot of requirements, or when we ask for something it's easier to get a yes. But I usually just act first and ask permission later."

And after several years with the new superintendent, Principal Jones can feel the change, which he described as follows:

> It took some time, but now it's becoming more of a partnership where I work with central and they really push my thinking about what kind of staffing this school needs and then they actually help me get those people. We can now opt into PD [teacher professional development], but what they offer is helpful so we use it more now than when we

had no choice. I put in the request today for someone to clear that graffiti, and guess when they are coming? Today! And I used to never see my supervisor except to do the required meetings and school visits for the principal evaluation. Now they are helping me focus on my instructional leadership. They connect me with my principal colleagues so we can learn together.

As these examples suggest, you would be hard-pressed to find a school district superintendent who does not have a vision that includes equity, usually in the form of a broad commitment to address long-standing disparities in school-related opportunities and outcomes for students identifying as Black, Indigenous, Latinx, students of color, or students affected by low-income circumstances. Their focus on equity seems promising because districts historically have advanced policies and practices that have perpetuated inequities.[2] Some superintendents are even cut from the same cloth as Principals Torres and Jones. Those leaders of color have devoted their careers and lives to racial and social justice and know well how the roots of educational inequities run deep—penetrating the daily operations of school districts in seen and unseen ways. Many seek the superintendency to disrupt those patterns and create new ways of working systemwide, with support for equitable teaching and learning at their core. Still, many of those visions play out like the one in Principal Torres's district. Superintendents change central office positions, titles, and people, but the day-to-day experience of school principals, teachers, and students largely does not change, and inequitable teaching and learning persists.

Some district leaders, like Principal Jones's superintendent, have bucked these trends and aimed to transform their central office. "Transformation" was their word. One superintendent told us, "When I arrived . . . it was clear that our goal had to be nothing less than a total district transformation." Another explained, "We are . . . trying to transform the culture of the district and schools . . . [to] focus on instruction and equity. . . . It's a shift in . . . culture . . .

saying that's [instruction and equity] what's most important." According to a third superintendent, we aim "to retool the entire district to support equitable instruction and leadership in the buildings." And a fourth described that central office transformation isn't a policy or program. "It's about rooting out racism and laying down new roots."

These leaders were concerned that their central offices were so misaligned with what truly advancing equitable teaching and learning required that they aimed to demolish and rebuild their central offices with support for equitable teaching and learning at their core. What they were doing was not the basic kind of central office "reorg" that is a typical approach of new superintendents like the one Principal Torres described. Common central office reorganization strategies tinker with titles and offices but tend not to transform how central offices actually function fundamentally—what staff do every day and how policies and systems operate—to support equitable teaching and learning in schools.

Instead, these superintendents and their leadership teams were starting sometimes literally with a blank page and asking, What if we could set our current central office aside and start from scratch—build a central office that, from day one, was designed to support equitable teaching and learning in schools as its essential purpose? And what if we did not start with the current organizational chart but first identified the *right work*—what a central office does when it supports equitable teaching and learning—and organized from there to reinforce that work?

For almost two decades, we have learned from and alongside central office leaders and staff members asking those questions and designing and implementing what we call central office transformation for equitable teaching and learning—*fundamental, aligned shifts across their central offices to support high-quality instruction and learning experiences in every classroom, every day, that center, value, and nurture the knowledge, cultures, and success of students who identify as Black, Indigenous, Latinx, students of color, and students affected by low-income circumstances.*

Using extended cases and detailed examples, each chapter in this book elaborates specific shifts in key central office functions—Teaching and Learning, Human Resources, principal supervision, operations, and the superintendent's cabinet—that our research associates with improved support for equitable teaching and learning in schools. Those shifts varied by function. For example, our data show how staff in Teaching and Learning pivoted from requiring that all teachers participate in specific professional development activities to elevating the leadership and professionalism of teachers to lead their own learning toward a common vision. Human Resources eliminated red tape and significantly built their capacity to partner with principals to ensure teacher success. Principal supervisors went from mainly evaluators, compliance monitors, and operations case workers to dedicated coaches of principals' instructional leadership. Operational units improved their efficiency and also provided new lines of service that enhanced students' learning experiences. And cabinet leaders dedicated their time to nurturing the leadership of their staff members and the cabinet itself to advance the work.

Our findings demonstrate that central offices *can* lead for equitable teaching and learning and that doing so requires fundamental systemic change. As we will elaborate in chapter 1, the changes were *fundamental* because they shifted the core premises—the basic assumptions and values—underlying each central office function to center new ways of working in support of equitable teaching and learning. The changes were *systemic* because they were not about improving one or two central office functions but all the functions across the entire central office in alignment with each other and in mutual reinforcement of the new premises.

In the final chapter, we discuss how central office leaders can use the findings to seed the design and implementation of central office transformation in their own districts in ways that build on the latest knowledge in the field; avoid predictable missteps; and, from that foundation, build the kinds of central offices we need to advance equitable teaching and learning. We urge policy makers, funders, and others to invest in central offices and their transformation to become engines of equitable teaching and learning. Doing so does not require significant levels of new funding that the word "transformation" may signal because much of what we discuss involves central office staff members eliminating old work and replacing it with the right work. Transformation does demand new imagination and support to set long-standing work aside and to take the kinds of risks that are unavoidable when dismantling the status quo and truly centering equitable teaching and learning.

HOW DO WE KNOW?

As we elaborate in the note on methodology provided in this book, our data come from ten US school districts ranging in size from 2,000 to 200,000 students. Our presentations of findings are also informed by our experience partnering with school district leaders across the country, helping them use ideas from our growing research base to develop their own approaches and shine new lights forward.

In our empirical work, we captured how district leaders and staff members evolved their work over time by embedding ourselves in it, observing almost 1,000 hours of meetings and events, talking to central office staff members in the office and during their commutes, and pouring over various iterations of documents that they created to evolve and solidify their new work. We did not rely on official statements of reform priorities or progress but focused on what we observed people putting into practice each day. We also examined data that leaders and staff members were collecting to gauge their progress, including principal and community satisfaction survey results and unit-specific performance scorecards.

Data reported by other agencies demonstrated striking improvements in our study districts, which corresponded with districts' engagement in central office transformation. For example, as central office transformation progressed in one district serving majority African American, Latinx, and Asian students, the percentage of schools receiving mostly A grades on their progress reports (which tracked indicators related to student achievement, student growth, and school environment) increased from 27.6 to 45.1 percent, and the number of schools receiving an "outstanding" or "well developed" on an external quality review increased by 25 percent. Another district was ranked by their state department of education as the most improved of the larger districts in their state for six years running, corresponding with their central office transformation efforts. A third district posted consistent gains on the National Assessment of Educational Progress (NAEP) and their graduation rates over nine years. And a fourth district saw graduation rates increase for seven years, with students identifying as Black/African American in the class of 2020 graduating at their highest rate ever—88.7 percent, a twelve-point gain over the previous year.

Such trends suggest that districts' central office transformation initiatives may have contributed to developments in schools that supported those results. However, available methods do not allow us to claim that the specific daily work changes involved in central office transformation caused them. Instead, we distinguished which central office changes to highlight in this book by first comparing what we observed central office leaders and staff members doing with practices and conditions that extant research suggests support equitable teaching and learning. For example, decades of research on adult learning shows that teachers and other professionals do not deepen their ability to teach for conceptual understanding through the typical mode of teacher professional development in districts such as one-size-fits-all workshops delivered to teachers outside their daily work. Instead, teachers and others do so when they have opportunities to engage in new practices in real situations in real time with colleagues similarly focused on learning those practices.[3] When central office reforms aimed to pivot to the latter mode of teacher development, we viewed those efforts as consistent with supporting equitable teaching and learning. Also, for example, research on culturally responsive teaching underscores the importance of curriculum materials and teaching strategies that *center* the experiences of historically marginalized students rather than adding consideration of those students and their cultures to otherwise unchanged core curriculum and definitions of high-quality teaching.[4] We cast central office change efforts that reflected the former approach as aligned with advancing equitable teaching and learning.

In some cases, implementation of central office transformation had progressed enough for us to substantiate our theoretically grounded conclusions further with empirical data demonstrating important results. For instance, our claims about positive and negative forms of principal supervision in chapter 4 are supported by our empirical data about principals' engagement in instructional leadership. Principals in our sample who deepened their engagement in instructional leadership tended to have principal supervisors who took a teaching-and-learning approach to principal support; principals with low or declining engagement in instructional leadership typically had principal supervisors whose practice reflected a traditional supervisory stance. Because these findings also reflected the robust research on assistance and apprenticeship relationships, we characterized the former cases as positive and the latter as negative.[5]

In addition, some operations units had their own data that demonstrated positive results. For example, one operations team tracked how much time their transformation efforts saved school principals and argued that principals could have redirected that time to their instructional leadership. Two operational units pulled themselves out of persistent budget deficits and pointed to specific general fund dollars that shifted from addressing their deficits to instructional support. Given the clear connection between the shifts in operations and improved support for equitable teaching and learning, we report those shifts as positive examples in chapter 5.

ABOUT THE CHAPTERS

Before we share those and other results, in chapter 1 we first frame our findings by explaining why superintendents were getting it right in calling for central office transformation for equitable teaching and learning. We show that extant educational research reflects a clear consensus that high-quality, culturally responsive teaching is essential for ensuring students' school success, especially the success of those students that public school systems have historically marginalized. School principals support such teaching when they operate as able instructional leaders. But realizing such teaching and leadership requires central office support that in the past has been short-lived or not provided at all. These results are not surprising given the history of central offices as agents of compliance, basic business functions, and the assimilation of students—and not as agents of teaching, learning, and equity. Even recent equity-focused reform strategies tend to tinker with not to transform central offices in the ways that realizing equitable teaching and learning requires.

Next, we identify the new premises common across our study districts that anchored their overall transformation efforts:

- The essential purpose of central offices must truly be to drive equitable teaching and learning districtwide.
- Everyone matters to realizing equitable teaching and learning.
- Transformation requires not a top-down or bottom-up approach but a partnership with principals.

In chapters 2–6 we detail specific changes in main central office functions that we associated with improved support for equitable teaching and learning. We grouped findings by function rather than department because our findings held across districts with these functions organized in various organizational configurations and staffing patterns. For example, in chapter 2, we address the teaching-and-learning function of central offices, including adoption of curricular materials and programs, teacher professional development, and school improvement planning across funding streams. In some districts, all those functions are in a formal Teaching and Learning (T&L) department or, in smaller districts, under the purview of the same one or two staff people. But in other districts, Human Resources (HR) conducts some teacher professional development, and Title I and other federal categorical programs are in separate offices. Because the positive findings about nutrition services, transportation, and custodial services were similar across all those operational functions, we discuss them together in chapter 5.

We begin each of these main chapters with a research-based vignette that describes the experience of a school principal in a district realizing all the improvements highlighted in the chapter. Each district was at varying levels of design and implementation of those improvements, but we compiled them into a single example to help readers see the big picture. Then we identify specific limitations of long-standing ways of working in each area that district leaders and staff members aimed to change. Next, we organize our main findings around new unit-specific premises that leaders and staff members established, based in part on the overarching premises of central office transformation, to ground the transformation of each function. We identify and define each premise and share examples of how leaders and staff members put them into practice.

Specifically, the vignette that starts chapter 2 describes how, before central office transformation, T&L was riddled with incoherence, internal competition, and ineffective and limited support for teacher learning, with equity concerns added on rather than integrated into T&L's core work. During transformation, T&L leaders and staff members shifted their work to reflect the premises that T&L units advance equitable teaching and learning when they:

- Align and coordinate all their work to a common set of standards defining equitable teaching and learning with culturally responsive practices as integral parts.
- Help teachers collaborate with colleagues to lead their own learning throughout their day toward the district's common teaching-and-learning standards.
- Strategically broker and selectively develop services and materials.
- Differentiate and deploy services based on strategic leverage points for adult learning in partnership with school leaders.

We illustrate these premises in action with specific examples from our study districts that included, for example, how staff members created new professional growth and school improvement planning processes to support teachers' leadership of their learning. We conclude the chapter by pointing readers back to the vignette to notice how the shifts in T&L we describe in chapter 2 depended on aligned changes in other parts of the central office, especially in HR, which we turn to in chapter 3.

Chapter 3 begins with another vignette from the perspective of a principal, this time emphasizing challenges she faced with HR when trying to fill teacher vacancies, handle absences and teachers taking leave, and manage other routine processes. As HR transformation got underway, she experienced less red tape and a new line of support that helped her ensure she had the right teachers in the right teams for their success, with an explicit emphasis on fostering the growth and retention of teachers of color. Those and other supports reflected new premises that HR units advance equitable teaching and learning when they:

- Eliminate, streamline, and redesign routine business processes continuously to free school and HR staff time to focus on strategic support for equitable teaching and learning.
- Ensure that teacher recruitment and selection drive equitable teaching and learning.
- Partner with principals to staff teacher teams strategically, with an explicit focus on supporting the retention and success of teachers of color.

HR's ability to act on these premises depended in part on shifts in other parts of the central office, including principal supervision, which we turn to in chapter 4.

The vignette that begins chapter 4 illustrates how one school principal made demonstrable improvements in their instructional leadership in ways they attributed partly to their principal supervisor, who shifted from a focus on evaluation, compliance, and operations to supporting their instructional leadership growth. Those shifts reflected new premises that principal supervisors help principals grow as instructional leaders when they:

- Operate with a clear conception of their role as a dedicated support for principals' growth as instructional leaders.

- Support principals to lead their own learning as instructional leaders.
- Supplement principals' leadership of their own learning with one-on-one coaching and facilitation of principal learning communities from a teaching-and-learning stance.
- Receive support for their growth from their own supervisor from a teaching-and-learning approach.

We identify how the ability of principal supervisors to fundamentally shift their roles in ways aligned with those premises depended not just on their own supervisors but also on aligned changes in T&L and HR, as described in chapters 2 and 3, as well as on major pivots in operations, which we discuss in chapter 5.

The opening vignette in chapter 5 shows how a principal was able to enhance equitable teaching and learning at their school thanks in part to particular shifts in the operational areas of facilities, transportation, and nutrition services. Those shifts reflected new premises that operational units support equitable teaching and learning when they:

- Ensure routine services maximize school time and other resources for instruction.
- Engage with school principals and others as a strategic instructional partner.
- Invest in the leadership and growth of operational staff members to serve as strategic supports to schools.

For example, in realizing these premises in practice, custodians joined instructional planning meetings to help ensure that schools' physical environments supported instructional programs. Bus drivers proactively engaged with students and families in ways important to student learning. The members of nutrition services partnered with classroom teachers to embed learning opportunities into mealtimes. These changes in operations as well as other central office units took a particular kind of leadership at the superintendent level, which we address in chapter 6.

In the final vignette of the book, which opens chapter 6, we meet a principal supervisor while he is participating in his internship for his superintendent credential program. He explains that most people in his program complete their internship in their own district, but he sought out a superintendent in a district sixty miles away because of how the superintendent leads her cabinet to support central office transformation. That superintendent discontinued the long-standing practice in cabinet meetings of providing informational updates with some discussion of key strategies and a focus on external matters. The transformed cabinet operated in ways that reflected the following premises that cabinets advance equitable teaching and learning when they:

- Lead the ongoing development and use of a theory of action.
- Foster staff leadership and learning.
- Focus cabinet meeting time on strategy and learning.
- Bridge strategically to external and internal resources and buffer against distractions.

Chapter 7 elaborates how school district superintendents and other readers can use this book to build on the experience of transforming central offices up to this point, avoid predictable shortcomings in common central office reform approaches, and innovate from there to shine new light on how central offices advance equitable teaching and learning. We identify specific next steps for district leaders and how policy makers, funders, and others can support them in this challenging work.

We also emphasize that unraveling and reweaving the basic fabric of a decades-old institution like a central office takes time. Leaders likely to realize success with central office transformation will be those who keep that long view; they will invest in changes that may take some years to flourish while identifying small wins to keep them and their staff members motivated and producing important results for students now.

When is the best time to start this long-term work? The sooner leaders begin, the sooner they will realize the kinds of meaningful and lasting changes we share in this book. It is never the wrong time to do the right work.

CHAPTER 1

The Trouble with Tinkering

In this chapter, we put the work of our districts in research and historical context to explain why realizing equitable teaching and learning requires leaders to stop tinkering with and start transforming their central offices. We begin by defining the importance of equitable teaching and learning and how central office policies and practices have not supported those results; in some cases, they have impeded them. We argue that those results are unsurprising given the history of central offices as long-standing agents of compliance, basic business functions, and assimilation. As a result, schools now typically operate in central office systems that reflect a profound mismatch between what equitable teaching and learning requires and what central offices have been hardwired to do. Then, we distinguish central office transformation for equitable teaching and learning as a type of change involving fundamental and systemic shifts—changes in the foundational premises that drive central office policies and practices across the organization to foster teaching and learning that centers and embraces diversity as a learning resource for all students. But our review of common reforms shows central office leaders tend to tinker with rather than transform their central offices in the ways equitable teaching and learning demands.

By the end of this chapter, we hope readers will deepen their appreciation of the importance of central offices to equitable teaching and learning and the disconnects between how central offices have operated traditionally and what equitable teaching and learning takes. We aim to reinforce for readers that improvement is possible and that it will require fundamental systemic shifts—which we call central office transformation for equity.

WHAT IS EQUITABLE TEACHING AND LEARNING?

To answer this question, we draw on scholarship about teaching and learning for conceptual understanding as well as culturally relevant pedagogy. The latter includes research on "multicultural," "culturally responsive," and "culturally sustaining" teaching and curriculum.[1] While most of our districts did not use these terms, the kind of teaching and learning they sought to support reflected the interdisciplinary research in both areas—teaching and learning for conceptual understanding and culturally responsive pedagogy—on how students learn rigorous, standards-based content and the importance of consistently centering, valuing, and nurturing the knowledge, cultures, and success of students who identify as Black, Indigenous, Latinx, and students of color, as well as those living in low-income circumstances. We call the results they were aiming for "equitable teaching and learning."

Scholars vary in their treatment of these ideas, but generally agree on the following. First, consistent with broader advances in scholarship on teaching practice, teachers help students develop conceptual understanding across content areas when they intentionally create classroom and other experiences that immerse students in critical thinking, authentic applications of challenging ideas, and identity development as learners on a trajectory toward achieving mastery.[2] Such teaching engages students in progressively more complex tasks that develop students' procedural knowledge about how to perform those tasks as well as their higher-order thinking—their understanding of how and why to solve problems in multiple ways and their ability to transfer knowledge to new contexts.[3] Teaching for conceptual understanding also involves teacher-student and student-student interactions and talk that help students draw on and value their own and others' experiences and knowledge and develop their agency to lead their own learning.[4]

But the nature of pedagogical tasks, talk, and other strategies in US schools historically has elevated the knowledge, cultures, and success of White, upper-class, male students.[5] For example, curricular materials have focused explicitly and implicitly on the experiences of White people of European descent in history and literature, sometimes casting others as just that—"other" and therefore less than.[6] Gloria Ladson-Billings has long shown how teachers frequently share examples that resonate with White students, praise the behavior typical of middle-class students, and otherwise ignore, devalue, or disregard the cultural and knowledge resources of students of color.[7]

When students of color on average perform worse on standardized achievement tests, remedies tend to cast these students as suffering deficits or damage rather than addressing well-known cultural biases in the testing instruments and processes.[8] Countless interventions have taken race- and class-neutral approaches, calling for high-quality teaching and learning for all students, which has left the exclusionary nature of core curriculum, pedagogy, and testing largely unchanged.[9]

Attention to culture, then, cannot effectively be added to core teaching but must be integrated into it as an explicit part.[10] When teachers do so, they use classroom materials, routines, and practices that advance conceptual understanding while recognizing each student's culture and ways of knowing as assets for their own and others' learning; in the process, they create joyful and caring classroom environments, especially for historically marginalized students.[11]

HOW DOES EQUITABLE TEACHING AND LEARNING DEPEND ON PRINCIPAL LEADERSHIP?

School principals are vital supports to teachers in realizing equitable teaching and learning.[12] Various studies show how such support, which we and others call "instructional leadership," includes principals ensuring that teachers have guidance and time to work together on strengthening their teaching practice.[13] Principals also support teachers in realizing equitable teaching and learning by providing teachers with consistent, intentional, evidence-based feedback about their strengths and areas for growth in their practice.[14]

In addition, principals have helped teachers elevate and integrate students' diverse cultures and knowledge into their core teaching.[15] Principals have done so by using humanizing data and assessment practices that reveal, respect, and value students' different ways of knowing; amplify students' strengths; and model for teachers how to do so.[16] Principals who support equitable teaching and learning also routinely interrogate and reflect on how their own race, class, gender, and other positionalities influence how they lead, and they model for teachers how to do so as part of continuously improving their practice.[17]

Principals advance equitable teaching and learning by staffing their schools with teachers who look like and have had similar life experiences as their historically marginalized students. Those teachers tend to hold students of color and White students alike to rigorous standards and recognize that each student has strengths as a learner, both of which are important to advancing student learning. Principals ensure that their schools have those teachers by actively recruiting and selecting them and placing them in positions and on teacher teams that are especially likely to support their retention and success.[18]

WHAT DO CENTRAL OFFICES HAVE TO DO WITH IT?

When we ask school principals how their central offices can help them lead for equitable teaching and learning, they often reply with a variation of the following: "They can get out of my way." When we probe a bit deeper, they say that they would welcome more central office support, but those wishes have gone unfulfilled for too long.

The experience of these principals reflects the limited but consistent research on educational equity that shows central offices generally have not supported equitable teaching and learning and, in some areas, have perpetuated inequities. For example, in her classic study, Jean Anyon chronicled daily racial discrimination and low-quality teaching in Newark, New Jersey, schools as a symptom of inequities stemming from the political economy of cities, including how public agencies like school district central offices operated, that were mirrored in school principals' resource allocation choices and teachers' interactions with students.[19] James Wright and colleagues have shown how central office decisions about school funding and closures can systematically disadvantage majority African American schools.[20] Other scholars do not name central offices specifically but trace the roots of inequities to key central office functions such as curriculum and instruction, teacher and leader training, data and assessment, discipline policies, school boundary setting, and family engagement, among others.[21]

Together, these findings reveal that inequities are rooted in central offices in ways that are both systemic and fundamental. Systemic problems are those that permeate multiple parts of an organization like a central office, which is one way to summarize the findings above that show the myriad central office functions associated with inequities in schools. Those parts do not operate independently, despite some critiques of central offices as being siloed. Rather, those parts are interdependent and work together to maintain the status quo.[22] Our own studies have demonstrated how changes in any one central office function, like school enrollment or principal supervision, require aligned policy and practice changes in others.[23] Therefore, tackling how central offices perpetuate inequitable teaching and learning in schools requires coordinated shifts throughout the central office.

The ways that central offices perpetuate inequities are not only spread across their functions but deeply entrenched in them, so interrupting central office inequities also requires fundamental change—sometimes called "radical," "transformational," or "institutional."[24] With these terms, scholars mean that racism and other inequities take root in the often taken-for-granted premises or "unseen" underlying assumptions, values, and beliefs that drive educational systems.[25] Those premises define who a central office should serve and in what ways, who has power to allocate and receive resources, and whose knowledge and culture should be valued and unquestioned as the norm.[26] As noted above, in the United States, those assumptions have advanced the supremacy of Whiteness, not the value of racial or ethnic diversity or cultural responsiveness.[27]

The history of US central offices throws the fundamental, systemic nature of central office inequities into further relief. Central offices were established in urban areas in the early 1900s to bring ideas about bureaucratic efficiency to the running of public schools and to advance "centralization, supervision, and professionalism," not to support teaching and learning.[28] In rural areas, central offices formed with similar aims and an emphasis on managing then-new federal funding.[29] Across settings, central offices focused on mass schooling and assimilation, not diversity and cultural responsiveness.[30]

And for about their first fifty years, central offices built up their expertise with basic business functions such as managing enrollment and the regulatory work of ensuring proper teacher licensing and the use of funds and other resources. They did so in ways that further emphasized the value of Whiteness and upper middle-class status through the selection of curriculum, the testing and sorting of students, and the closing of African American schools during desegregation.[31]

In the 1960s and 1970s, federal and state policy began to amplify the importance of teaching and learning and attention to historically underserved groups through new funding for math and science and special populations such as students affected by "disadvantage" and those with "limited English proficiency."[32] Central offices responded, in part, by increasing the number of staff and programs related to teaching and learning. But they typically did so unstrategically, adding staff members and programs in a piecemeal fashion and in ways that further marginalized students of color and those living in low-income circumstances.

For instance, as Title I funds for students affected by poverty became available, central offices generally created new positions or offices to manage those funds. Funds for other "special populations"—including students from migrant families or Indigenous communities, those experiencing homeless, and students eligible for special education services, among others—typically generated at least one new position or, in smaller districts, loaded additional responsibilities onto existing roles. This process continued as districts received targeted funding for career and technical education and gifted and talented programs as well as reading; science, technology, engineering, and mathematics (STEM); and other content areas. Not surprisingly, by the 2000s, central offices of all sizes reflected what we call a "Frankenstein effect." They had added functions as policy priorities and resources emerged. But like Frankenstein, they typically lumbered along with little coordination within or across functions and with parts sometimes working against each other.

The misalignment between what central offices do and what equitable teaching and learning requires was further amplified during the COVID-19 pandemic when central offices closed school buildings and shifted to remote learning. Various analyses showed that historically marginalized students were disproportionately disadvantaged by a lack of access to internet connectivity and laptops, formal instructional time, and quality teaching.[33] Some of those students reported that they were better off learning away from school buildings, where they typically experienced implicit and explicit harmful biases in curriculum and instruction, discipline policy, and testing, among other functions within the purview of central offices.[34]

THE TROUBLE WITH TINKERING

Leaders in our districts did not necessarily know the research or the history, but they understood that the problems with their central offices supporting equitable teaching and learning ran deep— that inequities were so intricately woven into the institutional fabric of their central offices that typical reforms would have limited success. They saw how some staff members wrote off those problems as the norm or as inevitable and viewed "successful" strategies as those that helped staff members work around the hurdles rather than eliminating them. But when those workarounds left the problems unchallenged, they reinforced rather than resolved those problems over time and exacerbated inequities.

For instance, the head of Human Resources (HR) in an urban district said that if you are a school principal who knows which HR staff person to call, then you probably don't have problems with HR. But that system of workarounds is extremely inequitable, favoring principals who have had time to establish strong relationships throughout the unit. In that HR director's words, "Who are those principals? Usually your veterans, White, and in our higher-scoring schools . . . [which is] code for majority White and affluent schools."

Many leaders had also experienced the limitations of common central office reforms that involved what David B. Tyack and Larry Cuban lamented as tinkering—the rewriting of position titles and reporting lines or the addition of new programs and training without changing the premises or underlying values and assumptions at the core of how central offices work every day, which resulted in little meaningful change or improvement.[35] For example, one common form of central office tinkering is the "reorg," or the reorganization, of the central office staffing chart to feature new offices and positions and different supervisory relationships among staff members, often in the name of amplifying a superintendent's priorities and improving performance.[36] In the vignette at the start of the introduction to this book, Principal Monica Torres's superintendent used these strategies when he changed the Curriculum and Instruction unit to Learning, Leading, and Innovation and added an equity officer. Seemingly more ambitious reorg approaches assign staff members to serve particular schools in cross-functional teams, in larger districts sometimes relocating them to regional offices for physical proximity. But reorgs alone do not change the actual work that staff members do every day. Reorgs sometimes increase staff interactions with schools. In cases where that support is low-quality or otherwise not supportive, however, those strategies can leave school principals feeling like Principal Torres— that the visits take school staff members' time away from other matters, increase their stress, and ultimately provide few benefits.

Some district leaders pursue customer service training. The latter typically aims to identify and address inefficiencies in current central office work by reducing the number of steps required for key tasks and increasing staff pleasantness and responsiveness when responding to schools. These reforms, like the reorg strategies, may tighten up and otherwise tweak—but not necessarily transform—the status quo. As a chief operations officer explained, "Some people think it's [central office transformation] all about customer service or service with a smile. It's not some touchy feeling thing . . . 'Oh, let's be all nice to each other.'" She elaborated that responding to emails and phone calls kindly and promptly is important, but if staff members aren't doing the right work, "Who cares?"

Other reforms center equity as a main driver, but they also tend to tinker rather than transform. For instance, an entire industry has emerged around equity audits.[37] These audits frequently involve an external team reviewing district policies, budgets, and other documents; interviewing staff members; and identifying areas for improvement. We find that many equity audits result in long lists of recommendations in the form of policy changes, resource allocation shifts, and training rather than a more substantial rethinking of a central office's core work. Many of the recommendations we have reviewed do not rest on clear evidence that making the changes will advance equitable teaching and learning. District leaders tell us that sometimes the list of recommended changes is so long that many go unaddressed. When staff members feel like the audit has been done *to* them rather than *with* them, they may lack the motivation to take next steps.

Some districts have appointed equity officers and offices to drive equity-focused changes throughout their central offices.[38] These additions to the organizational chart can signal a superintendent's elevation of and commitment to equity matters. But appointing individuals or units to affect fundamental change systemwide has had limited success in central offices and other contexts. For example, our previous research showed such strategies were ineffective at realizing even discrete, relatively technical central office changes in part due to the complexity of how multiple central office policies and procedures held the status quo in place.[39] Reports from equity officers suggest that, instead of using them as change resources, some central office staff members have deferred equity matters to them.[40]

Leaders in some districts invest in antibias training for their staff members as a cornerstone of their central office change strategies. With this approach, leaders posit that, if they shift the mind-sets and beliefs of individual staff members in ways that center, value, and nurture the cultures, knowledge, and success of historically marginalized students, then staff will work in ways that reflect that stance.[41] Other research supports that theory by highlighting how central office staff members' prior knowledge and beliefs constrain ambitious reform.[42] But changed minds do not always translate into action. Even new central office staff members with nontraditional backgrounds may, over time, operate as agents of the very systems they originally planned to dismantle.[43]

In addition, some district leaders have turned to design approaches that promise to help them generate new solutions to persistent problems. User-centered design, improvement science, and design-based implementation research (DBIR) now have track records of success.[44] We have observed many central office staff members using these methodologies to address discrete problems of practice, though, and not the premises that drive them, which can result in a game of whack-a-mole in which solving one problem exposes or creates other problems and leaves leaders in an endless cycle of problem solving.[45] Some applications of improvement science and DBIR have participants adopting, replicating, and fine-tuning existing solutions in local context rather than pushing toward the transformational shifts that equity requires.[46] Many design protocols we see in use in central offices do not prompt participants to center equity or confront and manage the inherent challenges of addressing institutionalized racism specifically.

A NEW IMAGINATION

As noted above, the leaders in our partner districts did not pull out a new organizational chart, training strategy, policy, or position but essentially a blank page. Over several years, they evolved fundamentally new and aligned approaches across their central offices that aimed to realize equitable teaching and learning. A blank page alone is insufficient, however, for bringing a new imagination to a century-old public bureaucracy like a central office. We sometimes give district senior leadership teams clean sheets of paper and ask them to sketch a central office that reflects how they think their central office should operate to support equitable teaching and learning as its central mission. Their portraits almost invariably reflect minor variations on their current central office. That tendency makes sense. Many central office leaders have risen in their systems' ranks for their expertise with the status quo, and many have not experienced different or better forms of central office work or other sparks to light their imagination.

The district leaders in our research were able to bring a new imagination to their central offices in part by starting with a few new premises about how their central offices should work and engaging staff members and others as essential partners in using those premises to rebuild their own work. We identified three main premises common across our districts that served as initial seeds for the specific changes, which we detail in the next chapters.

For one, *the essential purpose of central offices must truly be to drive equitable teaching and learning districtwide.* That premise meant moving staff members well beyond the general rhetoric that everything they do should be "for students" or "for all students." One central office leader explained that such shifts in language never really changed "what staff do and how they do it." Instead, staff members were to ensure that their daily work demonstrably built the capacity of schools for equitable teaching and learning in every classroom every day. This premise also meant many staff members had to stop leading with compliance and instead, organize their work around equitable teaching and learning first and then check for compliance or question the rules.

Two, *everyone matters to realizing equitable teaching and learning.* This premise aimed to interrupt the long-standing belief in some central offices that staff members in the Teaching and Learning or academics unit focused on equitable teaching and learning, but all the rest—business services, facilities, nutrition services, and, in some places, Human Resources—were on what some called "the operations side of the house" and not included in teaching-and-learning improvement efforts. Instead, according to a chief of staff:

> The reform is to ensure that all students—*all* students, not just pockets of students, which is what we've had in the past—that all students obtain knowledge that allows them to be successful to continue to matriculate through graduation and be college ready. . . . Whether they choose to go to college or not. . . . And that means . . . we are doing everything that we possibly can to support equitable teaching and learning in the schools. . . . That we understand . . . that our *only* reason we're existing is to ensure that our schools do [that] well. That is it. There is no other reason. And if you don't buy into that, you need to go work someplace else.

And "all" meant "all," including staff members on the "Teaching and Learning side." Those staff members ostensibly focused their work on teaching and learning, but according to the first premise and the history of central offices outlined above, they were not necessarily doing the right work to support it or *equitable* teaching and learning specifically. In fact, some of the most sweeping changes we observed during transformation in our study districts were in Teaching and Learning units.

Three, *transformation requires not a top-down or bottom-up approach but a* partnership *between the central office and school principals.* With this premise, leaders acknowledged the limitations of traditional top-down reform approaches where the central office largely directed schools' improvement agendas and actions. They also were not embracing so-called bottom-up, decentralization, or autonomy reforms that often called on central office staff members to take a back seat to schools and deliver mainly what schools asked for. Instead, transformation was about central office staff members and principals pooling their experience and expertise and working together to realize the common goal of equitable teaching and learning.

The "all" in the second premise, then, also included school principals. A central office leader with a business background explained:

> You have to change the whole mind-set of central office, but not *just* of central office. You also have to change the mind-set of the principals. About how they view our role and what the bigger picture is. . . . And that's a different shift. When I got here, people felt like, "Well, central office just has to make all the changes and the schools could just be the beneficiary of those changes." But everything that we do is an end-to-end process. So whether it's hiring a teacher or doing your school site plan or—take anything that we do. . . . Usually the process doesn't start in central office [but with principals]. . . . When you do process redesign, you have to look vertically, not just horizontally.

District leaders did not establish and direct staff members to use these new premises. Instead, as noted in the following chapters and emphasized in chapter 6, they engaged staff members individually and in teams over time to understand the premises and other aspects of their district's approach to central office transformation, scrutinize their current work, and identify promising new directions that reflected and, in some cases, extended beyond the premises in promising ways.

What did those promising new directions look like? We provide detailed answers to that question in each of the next chapters, starting with fundamental systemic shifts in the central office Teaching and Learning function in service of equitable teaching and learning in schools.

CHAPTER 2

From Delivery to Development in Teaching and Learning

"NICE WORK. MEETING ADJOURNED!" Washington Middle School Principal Michele Tatum said with a smile as she looked around the table. Her Instructional Leadership Team (ILT) of teachers and staff members just completed their final progress review of their school improvement plan (SIP) for that year. The entire team agreed that, only two years into the new SIP process, they already better understood their school's strengths and areas for growth and how to support teacher and student success. Principal Tatum explained:

> The old SIP was supposed to help us improve, but it was paperwork, not a process. I just took it home and got it done. It was plans for one year and due in October—so really like eight months. But it didn't matter because we sent it in and then set it aside. Didn't look at it again. The equity parts? Those were "Look at your test scores about how you keep failing your Black and Brown students and tell us what you plan to do about that." No feedback. No support.
>
> Now, the SIP gets us to look at ourselves and plan for the next *three* years and work back from that—which has really changed our thinking because the most important work takes *time*. Now we use data that really helps us know our students—student work, students' own

voices—always centering our historically marginalized students. Then, we work with T&L [Teaching and Learning] and HR [Human Resources] and figure out how to make it real. We look at: Do teachers have the materials they need? Do we have teachers on the right teams for their success? What PD [professional development] would help? How are we doubling down on the retention and success of our teachers of color? And we do it together. Me and my staff and central office, together.

What Principal Tatum describes is a fundamentally new way of working with T&L—the central office unit that typically handles school improvement planning, teacher professional development, and curriculum. In the past, T&L largely recorded completion of school improvement *plans* rather than supported school improvement *planning*. T&L mainly pulled teachers out of their classrooms for mandatory, one-size-fits-all workshops that were not consistently aligned to what Principal Tatum's teachers needed. The timing of the workshops—often during the regular school day—meant that schools depended on substitute teachers to cover classrooms. Tatum explained, "Subs are always a crap shoot. We missed too much quality instruction because my teachers were out learning how to provide quality instruction." Behind the scenes, T&L staff members competed for the limited number of days on the PD calendar in ways that led to spotty support in some areas. T&L provided curricular materials, but Tatum's teachers had to supplement them to fit the specific needs of Washington Middle School's students.

Now, teacher PD starts with teachers using a professional growth planning process to analyze the quality of their own teaching in relation to the district's strategic plan and instructional framework, a set of research-based standards defining high-quality teaching. Teachers use evidence of their current practice to set meaningful growth goals and to develop individual and team learning plans to help them lead their own learning largely throughout their regular school day and more intentionally during dedicated professional development time.

The process centers historically marginalized students in various ways. For example, the instructional framework integrates culturally responsive teaching practices into the core definition of high-quality teaching that teachers use to anchor their learning planning. Prompts guide teachers to monitor their growth continuously along those and other standards with evidence of how they are valuing and nurturing the cultures and knowledge of historically marginalized students as resources for their own and others' learning.

Principal Tatum said that teacher buy-in "skyrocketed" when they saw how the professional growth process helped them inform their own end-of-year evaluations with data they had collected themselves. She said that it also helped that the new SIP process started with their plans—first asking the ILT to review the teacher team plans with a focus on providing teachers with feedback and celebrating their success, and then building their schoolwide professional development to support those plans.

As part of that alignment process, ILT members consulted with HR and T&L staff members and Principal Tatum's supervisor to match staffing and PD to the school's needs. For example, at one meeting, the group discussed how seventh- and eighth-grade teachers had requested significant support with the district's new English language arts (ELA) curriculum. Together, they considered restaffing those teams so that each had at least one teacher experienced with the curriculum who could help lead team learning in that area. Because opportunities to restaff were a few months away, they instead reviewed the language arts PD packages available from T&L, chose one that fit their current needs, and planned for implementation.

The associate superintendent for Teaching and Learning reflected on the changes:

> PD used to follow test scores. Low scores, more PD. But there was a lot of great teaching happening in low-scoring schools and not-so-great teaching in high-scoring schools. So it got backwards. Then, too much PD got done *to* teachers. Teachers have to *own* their own learning and success. Teachers improve when they walk down the hall to consult with a colleague, not when they drive downtown to sit in this one chair all day. And we treated equity like it was something to take care of in a workshop or two instead of a wholly new approach to our materials, what counts as good teaching, the whole thing. Now, it's about asking, "What's happening at this school that is contributing to even one child not meeting their potential?" Then, "How can we really know

that school so that we are in a position to make some good bets?" Like if we go deep with teachers in these few key areas, that will matter beyond those areas. If you want to help someone learn, you create opportunities to truly focus. And that's what we are doing.

Principal Tatum's experience illustrates what our research shows about how central office T&L functions support principals and schools in building teacher capacity for student success.[1] We found that T&L does so by elevating teachers' leadership of their own learning toward common, districtwide standards defining equitable teaching and learning through processes that support individual, teacher team, and school-level adult learning planning. T&L also can support implementation of those plans through aligned professional learning opportunities and new attention to staffing. However, central office T&L functions generally have not worked in these ways. More specifically, what are the long-standing ways of working in T&L that district leaders aimed to interrupt? Which new premises anchored their T&L transformation efforts? How did districts realize those premises in practice? We address those questions in the following subsections.

LIMITATIONS OF LONG-STANDING WAYS OF WORKING IN TEACHING AND LEARNING

Across our districts, leaders were concerned with particular limitations of how T&L functioned. Those limitations included siloing, as well as the ineffectiveness of their equity and professional learning approaches.

Siloing

District leaders frequently lamented what some referred to as siloing within T&L—limited coordination and collaboration and heightened competition across staff and initiatives. In the larger districts, dedicated staff supported single-subject areas like mathematics or ELA, or specialized in student populations such as students affected by poverty, English language learners (ELLs), and children of migrant workers. These staff members had few incentives or opportunities to work together to support schools strategically. As a director of T&L in one of these districts described, "When we first started [central office transformation], there was a bizarre silo system where we were told, 'Don't talk to anybody, just sit there and work.'"[2] They recounted conducting an audit of T&L's functions:

> Trying to figure out what people do. What they think they should be doing. What they actually do. . . . Number one, [we found that T&L had] 100-and-some-odd coordinator types . . . people running around outside the classrooms and outside the schools. A lot of fragmentation. A lot of redundancy. A lot of the left hand doesn't know what the right hand is doing.

In smaller districts, where the same person was responsible for multiple content areas and programs, staff members still tended to provide support in those areas and programs separately. A T&L director in one of those districts described that T&L was full of initiatives "that I've inherited. They are here because there is a funding source and compliance attached. . . . Each one operating in its own silo."

Siloing created various challenges for schools. One T&L director described that her elementary school teachers had long experienced potentially complementary initiatives across subject areas as incoherent because her teachers were interacting with multiple, separate workshop facilitators and coaches who did not communicate or collaborate. She said, "They [the facilitators and coaches] don't get paid to do that and there's [been] no directive to work together, and we know coherence only happens when we all are saying the same thing to the same teacher." Typically, "[one program's facilitators or coaches] could be doing something in math and [another set is] with that [same] teacher in English language arts," with no collaboration across the two. One principal wondered, "Teachers have an inquiry process for math and now science and ELA too, each a little different. And do they really need all three?"

The lack of coordination and collaboration among coaches specifically also created various logistical challenges for schools. As a

T&L director in a small district described, schools are dealing with so many initiatives that they cannot always track their coaching and other centrally provided PD, and they sometimes lose teacher learning time as a result:

> And so then the coach [arrives at a school and] has to try to find the principal who may or may not tell [teachers the coach is coming] because he or she may not know. [The coach has to] try to find a teacher who doesn't know why you're there in their classroom. We're wasting time and it's not clearly defined.

As these examples suggest, siloing sometimes translated into head-to-head competition across initiatives for the limited hours dedicated to teacher PD and for other resources, such as substitute teachers and stipends for teachers to attend off-site workshops. One T&L director said, "I hate August because it's become a grudge match. Everyone's competing for [teachers'] time. . . . We replicate so many things when we could combine them if we just worked together." For instance, in one district, teachers sometimes found they were required to attend two different PD sessions run at the same time.

Competition also meant that, as math, reading, or other areas rose on a superintendent's agenda, investments in those areas increased and test scores would sometimes spike, but often at the expense of learning in other areas. For instance, one district launched a major initiative to provide comprehensive PD to teachers in mathematics using state-of-the art methods, including job-embedded coaching, peer consultations, and deep analysis of student work and talk. Teachers who participated reported in surveys that they loved the PD and found it helpful. School board members and the local media lauded the T&L math team for their part in the district's significant gains on the state assessment of mathematics over three years. But to deliver such PD, the T&L math staff took the majority of days on the district's PD calendar and more than half the district's available substitute teachers. Outcomes in other areas, including literacy, were either flat or declining during the same period.

Equity Added Onto, Not Integrated Into, Core Teaching and Learning
Our district leaders were also concerned that their district's core curriculum and teacher PD tended to reflect a race-neutral approach. That is, T&L selected curricular materials and ran PD sessions that promised generally positive results but not necessarily substantially better school experiences for historically marginalized students, let alone equitable teaching and learning across classrooms. Many materials and sessions actually centered and elevated White culture and norms and, in some cases, systematically devalued others.

For example, one veteran principal explained that several years ago, T&L had adopted a reading curriculum with strong average results but not specifically for students like hers, the majority of whom received support for English language learning. The texts mainly featured White American and European authors and characters and did not cover themes related to her students' rich Latin cultures and experiences. She described how she and her teachers spent considerable time supplementing and otherwise recasting the materials and that her teachers' PD days were consumed with mandated sessions about curriculum and teaching strategies that her teachers were not using. She said, "I told them [my teachers] you don't have to go. I'll ask for forgiveness later." But that approach still left significant gaps in curriculum and support that her teachers had to address themselves, and she worried about the multilingual students at other schools.

In addition, many T&L units typically aimed to serve historically marginalized students through special programs such as those for limited English proficiency as well as for students living in poverty, with migrant families, or without stable housing. Students often received services through those programs outside their classrooms during regular instructional time, although that approach sometimes limited students' access to the very core curriculum the programs aimed to provide access to, as reflected in Principal Monica Torres's experience described in the introduction to this book.

For example, early in one district's transformation process, we visited a school where students sat in small groups in hallways to receive help with reading and math, even though they were missing main classroom activities by doing so. By contrast, another school's principal showed us how her paraeducators worked alongside multilingual students and some students eligible for special education services during core instructional time in students' regular classrooms. She said this strategy was a main contributor to her school's growth, especially in fourth- and fifth-grade reading. When we asked how she was able to integrate those services into regular classroom instruction, she offered an explanation similar to the principal above: "I don't ask for permission. I tell them [T&L] a lot of 'no.'"

Some T&L units had been offering workshops and coaching in culturally responsive teaching, but staff members added them to their longer-standing offerings, and those sessions competed with others for teachers' time and sometimes substitute teachers and stipends, as noted in the previous subsection. One T&L director illustrated this problem with an example of her predecessor's investments in equity, which mainly involved hiring a consultant to deliver teacher training: "Culturally proficient pedagogy is what he [the consultant] really does . . . and he's dynamite." But because teachers were already busy with other PD, the training was optional. "He had three teachers that have come to his workshops all these other times, and they had no interest in implementing his thing, but they got paid for a week of attendance, and so I began to feel really uncomfortable that we weren't doing a better job, and that's [the situation with the three teachers is] ridiculous. That's a waste of resources."

Another T&L director showed us her unit's PD offerings from a previous summer and explained the ineffectiveness of the add-on approach to teacher PD:

> Do you see what's wrong here? You have math PD over here and then culturally responsive teaching over here [in different sessions]. But we want to see culturally responsive teaching *in mathematics* . . . and we expected teachers to put that together when we didn't do it ourselves. When we separate the equity work, they [teachers]

separate it. But the people who know math were over here, and the know-how about culturally responsive pedagogy was new, and it's really easy to stay in our comfort zone.

Ineffective Support for Teacher Learning

As some of the examples above suggest, our districts' T&L units had not carried out one of their key functions effectively: supporting the professional learning of teachers. Part of the problem was siloing and limited integration of equity. But many leaders noted that, even if they had solved those issues, T&L's long-standing approach to teachers' learning did not actually support it in at least the following ways.

Overreliance on pullout PD. Like others across the country, the T&L units in our districts had long delivered PD to teachers in pullout mode: in formal workshop formats outside teachers' regular school day, often with a focus on teachers gathering knowledge to apply later in their classroom. For example, in three of our districts, T&L staff ran summer professional learning retreats where teachers rotated through sessions in a district training facility, school auditorium, or lunchroom to learn about various topics like the content of new curriculum and changes in assessments. Throughout the year, teachers left their classrooms periodically to attend PD sessions offered away from their school sites.

In addition, T&L sometimes deployed consultants or subject matter coaches to run workshop-style PD in school buildings. For instance, one principal showed us a previous year's calendar for early-release Wednesdays, which featured various guests meeting with their teachers all together after school on numerous topics. Leaders' expressed concern that this mode of PD consumed significant resources, as noted above, and yielded little evidence that teachers actually shifted their practice. In the words of one chief academic officer, "My [PD] staff are the best in the business. If you go to one of those trainings you know you are with a master trainer. This is how we've always done it and they have gotten so good at it. But we haven't seen the results." She elaborated: "We know you can't get there [to deep shifts in teacher practice] in these workshops but we've had them on rinse and repeat for so long it's the rut we've been digging."

The pullout PD also disproportionately affected schools in low-income neighborhoods which, in some of our midsized districts, were also serving large numbers of students identifying as Black, Latinx, and Southeast Asian. A principal in one of those schools explained that his student population meant that his school was categorized as "high-need" and therefore had to participate in various initiatives and programs, each of which had required his teachers to attend trainings or conferences. His school's chronically low performance on standardized achievement tests added another set of required PD. As a result, his teachers were "maxed out; it was too much." And his students spent more time with substitute teachers than students in higher-income schools. He added that sometimes he had trouble getting substitute teachers to cover classrooms; the best he could do was get "any adult," which led to missed quality instructional time for his students.

Provided in delivery rather than development mode. The PD provided by T&L also tended to position teachers as relatively passive recipients of content delivered to them by central office staff members and others on a schedule determined by the central office, which limited teacher engagement or agency in their own learning. A T&L director shared how, at one districtwide session, teachers were "just sitting there for a stipend. . . . The audience . . . isn't there to learn. That was very discouraging." Another T&L director explained:

> It's one of the biggest contradictions we live. . . . That teachers learn when *they* make that learning happen. Even in [formal PD] sessions, you have to create that [opportunity]. But what we do is we sit them in that chair and say, "Now listen to this. All these wonderful things I have decided you need to know." No wonder they disengage. . . . And how are we supposed to help teachers spark student motivation and learning [when our PD doesn't spark theirs]?

One principal described one of these sessions: "We [teachers and principals] came, we sat, we listened, we left. It was epic."

Leaders and others made similar observations of PD provided by coaches at school sites, whether schoolwide or with individual teachers in their classrooms. One central office staff person described how their coaches fueled a culture of dependency for outside support, noting that coaches become "a kind of crutch" that teachers tend to wait for rather than seeking out other support for their growth. And that dependency leads to lost learning opportunities because even in good budget times, "We're sticking somebody [a coach] in and saying, 'Go fix them. You have two hours a week for ten weeks.' It's minimal support." Leaders were also concerned that, where coaches were assigned to schools based on a school's low standardized test score results, teachers in those schools tended to view the coaches as punishment rather than as professional support, which may have further dampened teachers' active engagement with them.

Tiered and targeted by test scores, not adult capacity. In partial response to changes in federal policy with the No Child Left Behind (NCLB) Act of 2001, many T&L units differentiated the PD they made available to schools based on student standardized test scores. Lower-scoring schools typically received more PD than higher-scoring schools, and, in some cases, less choice as to whether their teachers would participate. But students' standardized test scores did not necessarily indicate the quality of teaching or what professional support teachers needed, which led to wasted resources and teacher time. As one T&L director explained:

> We've been able to place some high fliers [teachers] in our . . . [low-scoring] schools. But PD follows the scores. Even after NCLB eased up, we are still doing it that way. I told them, "Stop. Just stop [overloading teachers in particular schools with PD]." The principals don't want it. Meanwhile, I've got these schools over here that are high-scoring where teachers need help but, in this world, they aren't a priority.

A high school principal confirmed this situation:

> It took a few years, but now I have a solid core of experienced, highly skilled teachers in this building, which historically had

been the placement no one wanted. [It was] a revolving door of brand-new teachers, White teachers, people unprepared to love and nurture these kids. Test scores are still low, but you see that in neighborhoods impacted by poverty and racism. So now I've got what I need [in terms of the quality of my staff], but because of the scores, we are loaded with initiatives, and they all come with PD that my teachers don't need. I've been turning money away [because it comes with] too many strings [misaligned PD].

Limitations of professional learning communities (PLCs). Prior to the launch of central office transformation, most of our districts had developed an initiative to support teacher learning in PLCs. These initiatives commonly called on schools to create groups of teachers who would collaborate to improve the quality of their teaching and student learning. But directors, staff members, and principals tended to describe PLCs as opportunities for teachers to meet and plan, not necessarily learn together. In the words of one T&L staff member, "Teachers always worked in grade-level teams, so like third-grade teachers or the math department all together. Then we started PLCs and we said '[Teacher teams and departments] now you are a PLC!' Only, little changed."

A T&L director elaborated that PLCs provided dedicated time, often protected by the teachers' union contract, for teachers to work with colleagues on curricular planning—what they would teach—and some teams routinely examined student work together and calibrated their understanding of what kinds of student work met state curricular standards. Beyond those kinds of conversations, PLCs typically did not support teachers' collaborative learning about how to improve the quality of their teaching practice. He whispered, "We have bet a lot [on PLCs as drivers of teacher quality], and we have no evidence [that the quality of teaching is improving]."

One T&L staff person responsible for PLCs described his job as "a delicate dance." He elaborated that because PLC time was protected in the teachers' contract, T&L generally did not want to risk a contract violation by "even suggesting" how teachers use that time. In part as a result, the PLCs met as bargained—outside teachers' regular practice at set times each week and involved discussions of their work, not real-time opportunities to practice in ways essential to professional growth.

NEW PREMISES FOR TEACHING AND LEARNING TRANSFORMATION

In most districts, these challenges are so common and formidable that they are written off or accepted as the norm, and "successful" strategies are those that help staff members work around the hurdles. When those workarounds leave the challenges unchallenged, over time they can reinforce rather than resolve them.

Our district leaders aimed to overcome those challenges by forging fundamentally new approaches across main lines of work within T&L. Each district had particular priorities and opportunities for change, but leaders across districts pursued strategies that reflected several common new premises about how T&L advances equitable teaching and learning. As we will elaborate in this chapter, those premises posited that T&L units do so when they align and coordinate all their work with a common set of standards defining equitable teaching and learning with culturally responsive practices as integral parts, help teachers and schools lead their own learning toward those common standards, strategically broker and develop services and materials, and differentiate and deploy services based on strategic leverage points for adult learning in partnership with school leaders.

Align and Coordinate All Their Work to a Common Set of Standards Defining Equitable Teaching and Learning with Culturally Responsive Practices as Integral Parts

This premise called on T&L staff members to define shared targets that centered, valued, and elevated the success of historically marginalized students, and to use those targets to rethink their work within and across traditional silos. These efforts reflected the research on teaching and learning for conceptual understanding and culturally responsive teaching and learning that we reviewed in chapter 1 as well as scholarship on how adults learn. The latter shows that a clear, valued definition or image of the target practices that learners are working toward is essential to deepening their engagement in those practices.[3] Such definitions help participants see that their professional community values particular practices, which fuels learners' motivation for learning.[4] These images also help learners see themselves on a trajectory toward mastery—a form of identity development that deepens learners' understanding of what it looks like and means to engage in new practices as they envision themselves doing so.[5]

Leaders in our districts had already adopted teaching-and-learning standards as part of previous reforms. With the launch of central office transformation, they worked with staff members to ensure that they had the right standards to drive equitable teaching and learning. For instance, one district had been using the National Council of Teachers of Mathematics (NCTM) standards, which addressed learning for conceptual understanding. Those staff members then created a series of questions for teachers to ask while using the standards to ensure they did so from a culturally responsive approach. For example, one adapted standard read: "To what extent do I support students in constructing viable arguments and critiquing the reasoning of others *in ways that reflect I value each student's rich cultural heritage and ways of knowing and am supporting students in doing the same*" (italics ours to show text district leaders added to the NCTM standards). Staff members in another district collaborated with local university researchers to identify specific teaching practices that school and central office staff members would commonly seek to support using an extensive engagement process to elevate voices from historically marginalized communities as they did so.

Two smaller districts operated in a state that had required the adoption of a state-approved teaching-and-learning framework to anchor their teacher evaluation system. Both their superintendents emphasized the importance of their chosen frameworks focusing, in the words of one, "much further upstream," where we make sure "teachers have the materials and learning supports they need for a successful—really, a meaningful evaluation process." She elaborated:

We could have just sat here [in our cabinet meeting] and chosen one. We were already using [one of them] because of [our work with local consultants that developed one of the state-sanctioned frameworks]. But we said this is bigger than that. We can just rubber-stamp it, or we can do the deeper work of meaning making . . . [and] choose one that fits us [and] our kids and that unifies [us across silos] in a common direction, and if it doesn't, then address that head on.

We observed her facilitating one in a series of discussions with T&L staff members, principals, teachers, and community members to consider issues of fit. The superintendent opened the discussion about the framework's student engagement standards by saying:

[The standards] as is . . . [treat] student engagement as a universal thing . . . without really interrogating if the kinds of engagement the standards highlight are consistent with the cultures and values in our community. . . . If the standard sets expectations for your child that are not consistent with your values at home, it's on us [educators] to understand that and make sure your child is successful. [The purpose of the meeting is] to clarify what we in [the district] mean by student engagement, in all its forms, that reflects our diversity.

Participants then rotated around a series of stations, each of which asked them to think about their own child or one they knew well and what that child would be doing in a classroom if participating in ways consistent with a given student engagement standard and also their family and cultural values. After completing all rotations, participants chose one station, reviewed the input provided at that station, and identified recommended adaptations to the given student engagement standard.

In an interview, this superintendent elaborated, "Our [communities of color] did not want their children held to different standards . . . historically, different means lower . . . less than. They did want us to recognize that by their own cultural standards, their students might be highly engaged in ways the state standards didn't [help us see]. So we made sure we captured that [reflected those cultural differences in the version of the standards used moving forward].

Staff members in many districts also described and demonstrated how using the teaching-and-learning standards addressed problems with siloing. For instance, one T&L director convened her staff members in a series of retreats to examine the services they provided to schools against their teaching-and-learning standards. They found that, for years, they had allocated resources in ways that emphasized some areas over others—a dynamic they did not realize before the common standards helped them, in the director's words, "create a map . . . to truly see, really understand [ways they were leaving schools unsupported or overwhelmed]."

Another district's T&L director said that her unit always had a list of services they provided that the different subject matter teams "just pasted together . . . [with] no consultation or checking to see [what else was on the list]." As part of central office transformation, she worked with staff members across content areas to create what they called a "service menu" that displayed services by the elements of the teaching-and-learning standards they addressed. "It's like when you go to a restaurant or open a brochure. . . . You can really see what we offer." She elaborated that this exercise created transparency for schools about what to expect from T&L but that the "biggest benefit was for [T&L] staff. . . . It's such a simple thing. . . . Now they could open up the menu and see where they fit in, what everyone is doing. It's turned out to be pretty powerful in bringing us together."

For instance, such processes helped the T&L science and math staff members realize that they faced the same challenges with elementary and middle school teachers struggling to use critical questioning strategies in culturally responsive ways. They then worked together to construct a common series of question starters and other shared tools and began to consult routinely with each other on their progress with particular schools. One of these staff people described how she and her colleagues, "some I didn't even know before we started," convened regularly to revisit the menu's alignment with common priority areas. She said, "I think that, with the professional development, we're now all in the same place. . . . It [the teaching-and-learning standards and conversations we have about our work in relation to them] . . . unites us as one team."

And in the words of another T&L staff member, "At one time we were all using different instruments, but now we have a common set of standards [defining equitable teaching and learning] that all of us use—whether you're a principal, teacher, or central office executive director. . . . So everyone is familiar with that [set of standards]." Principals corroborated the positive effects of having such standards to ground the new work in T&L. As one put it, "This is one of the first times [in a long time] that we [are] all pulling the rope in the same direction."

Help Teachers Collaborate with Colleagues to Lead Their Own Learning Throughout Their Day Toward the District's Common Teaching-and-Learning Standards

This premise prompted T&L staff members to shift from mainly developing and directing mandatory teacher PD to helping teachers lead their own learning both individually and in learning communities during their regular workday in a common districtwide direction. One T&L director reflected on the importance and challenge of relinquishing a top-down professional learning approach in favor of helping teachers lead their own learning:

> Now we are saying our job is to help schools realize what they need and how they can drive [their own growth]. I am not coming up with solutions. . . . Sitting on my hands is *hard* because what I often have done in the past is gone in, assessed, and then created a training plan. . . . The hardest part . . . is helping the site understand the issues so that *they* can ask for [help].

Districts' efforts in this area were consistent with at least three key findings from research about how adults learn to deepen their engagement in challenging new practices. First, adults deepen their engagement when they have opportunities to exercise agency or leadership over their own learning.[6] When learning environments help learners grow and activate their agency, learners experience more motivation for and efficacy in deepening their practice than when positioned as passive recipients of information.[7] Agency also fuels learning by prompting learners to seek assistance and to practice even when an assigned coach or other mentor is not available.[8]

Second, many scholars have demonstrated how learning outside authentic settings (e.g., beyond the context of teachers' regular classroom teaching) can lead to superficial understanding and use of new ideas. Instead, learners deepen their ability to work in new ways *in practice* or by actually engaging in those new practices during the course of their regular work.[9]

Third, working within a job-embedded learning team, sometimes called a community of practice, helps learners engage in progressively more challenging professional work.[10] In a community of practice, learners at different levels of expertise work alongside each other, providing novices with opportunities to observe expert models and to develop conceptions of the target practices essential to their progressing toward them over time. In such communities, novices participate integrally in the growth of the community, which fuels their motivation, identity, and sense of efficacy for learning. At the center of communities of practice are clear, valued target practices that serve as vital learning resources, as noted above in the discussion of the importance of having common districtwide teaching-and-learning standards.

In practice, the T&L units in our districts significantly cut the time and resources they spent delivering and directing PD and created new tools, processes, and supports aligned with this premise. For one, several districts developed what one T&L leader called a *professional growth planning process*—a set of inquiry-based protocols that helped teachers self-assess their strengths and areas for growth along the district's teaching-and-learning standards and then develop plans to lead their own learning throughout the year. Some prompts in these processes asked teachers to consider which workshops and conferences they might attend. Other questions helped them explore on-the-job learning opportunities, such as collaborating with colleagues who could provide them with feedback and ways their grade-level team or other PLC could help advance their growth. Another T&L director described a similar process in their district:

> So you go in [to the inquiry tool] . . . you self-assess on what you've accomplished [toward] your goals along the competencies [elements of high-quality teaching and learning] . . . and that becomes the basis for your own development, which *you* own. That . . . system really helps penetrate the organizational DNA [get to the root of daily practices] . . . working toward goals and improving our capacity. Then, the idea is, in the spring, teachers can guide their own evaluations, much like we know to do with student-centered assessments.

Another T&L director said that it is one thing to want teachers to lead their own learning and engage in authentic learning with their peers, but without a clear sense of how to do that "[teachers] just kind of freeze, panic. And they're running around for a quick fix instead of taking the time to dig a little deeper for the root cause [of the quality of their teaching]." The professional growth planning process helps "to take them to a place where they can define what they need . . . to go on an inquiry journey a little bit." To support that inquiry journey, T&L staff members created a self-guided protocol to help teachers develop evidence-based learning plans and optional periodic workshops to review the ideas behind the process and provide teachers with feedback on their progress.

A chief academic officer explained, when he arrived, "If you said 'plan,' teachers heard 'punishment'" because, in accountability reforms over the previous twenty years, the word "plans" referred to plans for improvement for teachers with low marks on their annual evaluations. "So we had to do a lot of reculturing." The main strategy was "if you build it, they will come. . . . [We focused on] how do we create an inquiry process . . . [and a] set of inquiry tools that really speak to teachers and what they need." He elaborated that he and his team first made the materials available to teachers and gradually began integrating them into his staff members' PD sessions. For example, at the launch of a new program in social emotional learning, facilitators used self-assessment processes from the professional growth planning tool as main materials to activate teachers' agency in the trainings.

T&L units also developed a significant line of *support for teacher professional learning communities*. As one T&L director explained:

> Since any of us can remember we have had PLCs. . . . Now we are saying PLCs are the foundation. . . . Now we are saying PLCs are a main point of investment. . . . This is some of our hardest work because my staff says, "Oh that part [of central office transformation]? We do that already [support PLCs]." So I have to take them to a place where they can see you do and you don't [you have promoted PLCs but not teacher learning teams]. So teachers do and they don't [participate in authentic learning teams].

These investments included materials to help guide teacher learning teams. For instance, one T&L director worked with her staff over several months to create a rubric that defined developmental phases of authentic teacher learning teams and activities to help teams progress to later phases. In another, T&L staff designed protocols to help teacher learning teams self-assess their readiness to realize the student learning goals in their school's improvement plan and to develop intentional plans to learn together throughout the year toward those goals. One protocol's prompts asked teams to position particular members as facilitators of learning opportunities in which they were more advanced and to visit each other's classrooms as models and to provide feedback.

The investments also included new strands of professional development focused on developing authentic teacher learning teams. For example, leaders in one district held a series of voluntary all-district sessions with a national expert on teachers' collaborative learning. The purpose of the sessions, in the words of one leader, was to "lay a common foundation," including a districtwide definition of teacher learning communities. They followed up on that series by offering tiered packages of support that schools could choose depending on the degree of teacher team implementation. For example, an intensive package aimed to help novice teams build their capacity to learn together. A lower-end package focused on helping more mature teams monitor their own progress.

Two districts also launched major initiatives to redesign their *school improvement plan (SIP)* to reflect this premise and, in so doing, shifted their SIP from a compliance-oriented report to a process supporting teachers' leadership of their learning. As one T&L director explained, the "whole idea" of SIP redesign was "to have them [schools] build something that was more visionary and leading than procedural."

In this leader's district, the redesigned process first guided principals to collaborate with various stakeholders on the development of a three- to five-year vision for their school as a vibrant learning community reflective of the cultures of their students and neighborhood and aligned with the district's strategic plan. Teachers then worked individually and in teams to examine various data about their students (e.g., test scores, samples of student work, grades, classroom observations), to identify specific student growth goals and strategies to help them advance toward the vision, to assess their current ability to use those strategies while also growing along the district's teaching-and-learning standards, and to develop plans for learning together toward those outcomes. School leadership teams then reviewed the learning plans with an eye toward how they could provide schoolwide professional development and access support from T&L to supplement teams' efforts to lead their own learning.

In these districts, the redesigned SIP included various prompts for school staff members to center the experiences of historically marginalized students from a strengths-based approach as the basis for their learning planning. For instance, one protocol asked teacher teams to move well beyond test score data to consider a broader range of evidence that amplified each student's strengths, including those that may show up mainly in out-of-school settings. Another recommended that teachers engage in student shadowing and home visits as key data sources to, in the words of one, "move away from big data. . . . If you really want to see how the system operates, you have to walk around in . . . [one of our historically marginalized students'] shoes."

One of these districts integrated their separate processes for English language learning (ELL), Title I, and other categorical programs serving historically marginalized students into the new SIP process. As the chief academic officer explained, once they had the basic parts of the new system in place, we asked, "How [do] we integrate some of the other pieces we use around planning . . . [so] it [how we serve historically marginalized students] becomes naturally integrated [into core instruction]? . . . All these different plans [got in the way of that]. How do we really think about serving all of our students?"

For example, prior to the launch of a central office transformation, the head of ELL programs had typically guided schools in creating school-level teams to address supports for students eligible for those programs but in ways that were separate from the main school-level leadership team and SIP process. The redesigned SIP protocols now advised schools on how to ensure that their main leadership team was also compliant with federal rules for funding for English language learners and integrated prompts for the leadership team to consider research-based practices for supporting English language learning through core instruction.

Strategically Broker and Selectively Develop Services and Materials

With this premise, T&L staff members shifted further away from their long-standing mode of positioning themselves as the main developers and deliverers of teacher PD and curricular materials. Instead, they were building their capacity to broker services and materials from others actively and strategically. As we elaborate below, brokering involved curating resources from external and internal sources (e.g., schools), screening them for quality and fit, and making information about the resources visible to all principals and teachers. T&L staff members also developed services they provided themselves, but selectively—mainly to fill gaps and create continuity in teachers' and students' learning experiences. One way to think about this approach is that leaders saw T&L staff members as the PD providers of last resort.

Research on learning in communities of practice and other social settings underscores the importance of brokering activities, sometimes called boundary spanning, to ensure that learners have supports especially appropriate for their starting places and progress.[11] External boundary spanning helps communities access necessary learning resources not already in their community. But learning resources within a community may also go underutilized without internal brokering to identify those resources and put them into use.[12] The active curation, including translation and framing, of external and internal resources helps learners see their relevance to their own learning toward particular growth targets.[13]

In one district, for example, T&L staff members created a repository of online curricular materials and professional learning opportunities for teachers and other staff members that was aligned with their teaching-and-learning standards. The T&L director explained that many helpful resources were now available in open-source format online, and "it's a waste of resources to have teachers out there searching. And inequitable." She elaborated that veteran teachers had amassed various supports and materials for years, but newer teachers, who were mostly teachers of color, had not. One staff person in this district described interviewing veteran teachers about resources they found helpful and making that information widely available online.

In the district with the service menu, staff members actively searched for resources that were research-based. Their T&L director explained:

> We wanted to make sure . . . to bring what we know about research into practice. What we haven't done well as a system through the years is take research and say, . . . "This is research. It tells us this is what is good. Why are we not using it?" It's like [a reading program she pointed out on the service menu]. . . . Yes, it's an expensive model. But time and time again, research has shown that, if you sustain this over time, you will improve literacy.

Several districts also actively brokered resources internally. For example, two districts cultivated what one leader called "lab schools." Common features of those efforts included having T&L staff members and school leaders identify school communities that could serve as PD resources for others and helping them do so with incentives and administrative support. One T&L leader explained that the lab schools were an explicit part of their equity efforts. They gave an example of a school in a predominantly upper-middle-class White neighborhood that for years had built its capacity for high-quality reading and writing instruction and hosted teachers from other schools to learn with them. But the visiting teachers were mainly from similarly affluent neighboring schools that happened to know about the coaching opportunity. As part of the district's new lab school efforts, T&L staff members helped the mentor school organize and advertise the lab visits on the district's main professional development calendar and provided targeted outreach to schools in lower-income neighborhoods.

Brokering involved not only bringing resources in but also screening them out or buffering. A T&L staff person in a midsized district described this aspect of brokering: "People contact [the superintendent saying], 'We have this fabulous program. We wanted you to do it.' . . . Too often a lot of the vendors just see us as a cash cow and they try to bring in anything and we're supposed to . . . take it. [In this district,] it doesn't work like that." She elaborated that, in the past, central office and school staff members would just see how "it's a program coming out of Harvard so it must be good. . . . But we are already doing this for our teachers, and it was going to be an expensive program. Why pay for it when we are already doing it?" Similarly, a staff person in another district shared that some vendors had become "too comfortable" with their district contracts, providing the same services each year with little results. As part of the new brokering efforts in these districts, vendors had to provide evidence of effectiveness—either up front or shortly thereafter—and submit a plan for building the district's capacity and lessening reliance on the vendor. As she put it, "They need to tell us how they are going to put themselves out of business before we do business."

T&L staff members still developed and provided teacher PD and curricular materials themselves but selectively—supplementing and filling gaps in the resources they could access from other sources. Many T&L units redirected staff members from providing PD in particular subject areas to developing processes and support for professional growth planning, teacher learning communities, and school improvement planning. One T&L director explained that they not only found few external resources in those areas but that they wanted to demonstrate their commitment to teachers' leading their own learning by focusing their own staff members' efforts in those areas.

In one of these districts, the T&L director reconfigured his staff, first creating positions focused on providing support for teacher learning teams and other strategies for helping teachers lead their own learning. As a next step, he assigned staff members to curate external and internal resources by subject area. Then he considered what additional support the staff members would provide themselves. In his words, the latter included helping schools "coordinate the [brokered] services and create a coherent plan. . . . And we sometimes see that teachers need additional help. So we develop follow-up activities pretty much designed based on the needs of the school sites."

In one district that had begun to transform its SIP in the ways noted above, T&L staff members analyzed the new SIP reports as part of their efforts to better understand schools' goals, strategies, and areas for growth. In the first year, they focused on aligning the PD they provided with school goals. In subsequent years, as schools were able to identify gaps in learning resources themselves, T&L staff members prioritized those areas.

Differentiate and Deploy Services Based on Strategic Leverage Points for Adult Learning in Partnership with School Leaders

Districts' efforts to help teachers lead their own learning and to strategically broker and selectively develop services and materials, as discussed above, also reflected an emphasis on differentiation—T&L pivoting from a one-size-fits-all approach to teacher and school support to one that tailored support to teachers' and schools' growth areas.

Importantly, T&L units were not differentiating mainly by student test scores but by the learning needs of teachers and other school-based instructional staff members. In the process, T&L staff members aimed to be strategic—collaborating with educators in schools and across long-standing subject matter and program silos around questions such as: What are this school's most important gaps in their ability to lead their own learning? Of those gaps, which ones are key leverage points, areas in which improvements will also drive growth in other areas? And how can we connect the school with support to address those leverage points? As a T&L director in one district expressed:

> [This is the part] which I'm most excited about. Using data to really know what schools need beyond school types—turnaround school, high performing. Because those types of labels do mean apples and oranges, but not [a clear enough indication of] what support they need to succeed. We want to get much more refined in thinking about schools and in partnership with principals and teachers.

In the words of another director, "Everything that we're doing, it's about having a laser-like focus on where the children are [with their learning], which requires a laser-like focus on where the adults are."

These concerns also reflect research on learning, in this case, about the importance of differentiation to supporting professional growth.[14] Researchers generally define "differentiation" as the ongoing use of evidence to understand a learner's proficiency with a specific task or broader activity and, from there, the tailoring of assistance to each learner and situation.[15] The task-specificity of this definition is important because learners are never equally proficient in everything and benefit from different types and levels of support, depending on the situation. Some specify that differentiation that demonstrably deepens learning builds on learners' strengths to leverage their weaker areas and generally that adults grow in multiple areas by going deep in a few and transferring that learning to other areas.[16] The emphasis in the research on engaging learners in the differentiation process further reflects the research cited above on the importance of agency to learning.

In practice, some districts differentiated their T&L services by shifting from one-size-fits-all supports to those tiered by teachers' readiness. For instance, as noted above, one T&L unit developed "service packages" to support teacher learning teams that varied by team maturity. A T&L director described working with staff members to move in that direction:

> I said we're going to define our work just like we were going to do a brochure. And so we spent until January being very clean, clear, and precise about what the work is. . . . So that we can be consistent. . . . You [school principal] come in here, you pick this package, and now what we're going do is calibrate it [help you match it to teachers' growth areas].

As part of these sessions, this director had her staff members engage in role-playing activities, with some staff members posing as members of specific school leadership teams and others as T&L personnel. These conversations aimed to help staff members develop processes for working together with each school to pinpoint how T&L services could address specific strategic gaps in schools' ability to lead their own learning. In her words, "We created all these scenarios with real schools. . . . Those practices have transformed how we do our work, and when we got people well-trained, then we started seeing the benefits." She reported the following a year after launching those sessions: "We do far more collaboration with [school] sites to be more precise about what their needs are. A lot of conversation has taken place this year. We're not saying here are the three programs we are offering this year and you have to fit into this box. We're really negotiating."

T&L staff members in another district collected evidence to inform differentiation with a protocol for visiting schools that prompted them to ask principals and teachers questions to reveal key leverage points for support. This district's T&L director stated that the protocols meant that "if I'm going to go to your school, I am able to . . . interview you. . . . So that I've asked most of the possible questions that will help you get to the place where you can identify some of the causes [of the quality of equitable teaching and learning at your school]."

One of their counterparts in another district described creating a team of master teachers who visited schools to conduct what she called SWOT (strengths, weaknesses, opportunities, and threats) analyses where they go in and "see what they can see. . . . Not from the standpoint of catching them doing it wrong," but to help them identify resources for improvement and then gaps that their T&L department could uniquely address.

In a district where schools were required to choose whole-school reform designs (e.g., Expeditionary Learning Outward Bound, Success for All) to focus their approaches to student learning, T&L was realigning its services to match the performance demands they knew each design placed on teachers. In the districts that were transforming their SIPs to surface information about teacher capacity, staff members met in cross-subject-matter teams to analyze the new SIP reports together and make recommendations to principals about which professional learning options might leverage particular results.

SUMMARY

The premises discussed in this chapter seeded new ways of working across T&L functions especially in the areas of teacher PD, school improvement planning, and curriculum that promised to support the development of teacher capacity for equitable teaching and learning. Prior to these changes, principals like Michele Tatum were on the receiving end of mandatory PD, compliance-oriented SIPs, and curricular materials that did not always work well together, align with her teachers' needs, or help her make equitable teaching and learning her school's main business. With the new approaches, her teacher PLCs were becoming stronger learning teams with the tools and support to grow together in ways essential to their students' success. When she sat down to complete her end-of-year teacher evaluations, teachers shared their learning plans and evidence of progress that they had collected themselves and otherwise co-led the discussion. She and other principals increasingly viewed T&L staff members as partners in their common pursuit of equitable teaching and learning.

The ability of principals like Michele Tatum to develop strong teacher teams and otherwise support teachers' growth also depended on her school having the right teachers on the right teams for their success. The right teams were those with sufficient expertise to lead their own learning. The right teams were also configured with particular attention to ensuring the growth and retention of teachers of color. A principal's success with supporting teacher growth therefore also depended on specific shifts in how Human Resources helped her recruit, select, and place teachers as well as develop and retain them. We take up those shifts in Human Resources in chapter 3.

CHAPTER 3

From Staffing to Strategy in Human Resources

ROBIN GREENE, principal of Sound Elementary School, pulled out her planner from last year and said, "Look, I can show you." She was describing how much time she and her leadership team used to spend preparing for her school's annual spring budget and staffing meeting. She said:

> It was *hours*. And that's just what's on my calendar. All of that for one meeting—downtown with twenty minutes to share our wish list for staffing with central HR [Human Resources] and budget. We made our presentation. We looked at budget and vacancy projections. Which we had already sent in [to HR] so they already had it! And there is only so much you can do to build a staff opening by opening, retirement by retirement. But that's how we did it. And then, when an opening came up or enrollments shifted—Groundhog Day. We just had to go over it all over again.

But the district's HR transformation process made that meeting obsolete, and last year, the district canceled it. The HR director explained:

> My staff was drowning in processes that took multiple steps and, like the spring meeting? Totally unnecessary. Redundant. We stepped back and made an inventory of all our work processes and identified

what we can just stop doing or significantly trim down the steps. That literally wiped out about a third of our processes. Then we started to look more deeply at the processes that remained and how to redesign them in a way that made everything easier for principals and teachers and our own staff.

In tandem with that streamlining and redesign, a team of HR staff members, personnel from the Data and Accountability office, and a local university researcher worked together to develop a "teacher profile"—a set of standards that every new hire would have to meet to ensure that every teacher, from day one, was likely to be successful. That effort started with the standards of high-quality teaching and learning that the district's Teaching and Learning (T&L) unit had adopted to anchor professional development. The team then asked, "What experience must a candidate have and what competencies do they need to demonstrate at the point of hiring to increase the likelihood of their success along those standards?" To help them answer that and related questions, the team examined research and their district's own workforce data, which provided a set of initial predictors of teacher performance and retention. In the words of the HR director, "Now, you are a principal and you don't have to ask for teachers who have a basic level of cultural competency coming in or at least initial experience with ambitious mathematics instruction because that's our baseline. The goal is we won't show you a candidate who isn't already on that ground floor."

HR was also able to dedicate staff members to work directly with principals to use staffing as a main driver of equitable teaching and learning. Now HR partners collaborated with each principal to develop a strategic staffing model—an aspirational map of the experience and expertise they believed they needed on each teacher team to support teacher team learning, with an explicit focus on the success and retention of teachers of color. The superintendent summed up these changes: "Our HR unit used to staff vacancies. Now, they build teacher teams." She elaborated:

> Like a lot of districts, we have relied on PD [professional development] and PLCs [professional learning communities] for teacher support. But we weren't getting the results. In any other industry, leaders know that

performance starts with staffing strong teams. So then we started to say, "Any good PD starts with staffing, with making sure teachers are on the right teams so they can learn well together." But our strategy was still, "Okay, bam, those third-grade teachers are now a PLC and they have ninety minutes of weekly planning time. No further guidance or help." And as a district, we had too few teachers of color and what did we do? Principals competed for them, they got spread across schools, and ended up being the only teacher of color on their team and maybe their school. Which is basically exactly what *not* to do if you want to support and keep those teachers.

The strategic staff planning process at Sound Elementary School started with Principal Greene and her HR partner working through a protocol over several meetings that asked questions such as: Given the district's strategic plan and our schoolwide vision, beyond what's in the teacher profile, what is the expertise we need on each of our teacher teams to ensure they can learn well together? They also reviewed guidance that the HR partners and T&L staff had been developing about that expertise, such as the importance of dual-language schools having native speakers on each team and teachers who had participated in an intensive training program to lead teacher learning in inquiry-based science. In the process, they considered research such as that on the isolation teachers of color feel when they are the only one on their teacher team, which in turn can have a negative effect on their retention.

Then they compared Greene's current teacher teams with the forward-looking staffing model to identify gaps. They also looked at data on teacher performance and retention. That analysis revealed that the current fourth- and fifth-grade teams had enough expertise to grow their teaching along the new science standards, but in the earlier grades, 82 percent of staff members were humanities, not science, majors; those teachers had participated in science PD sessions, but classroom observations revealed that the teachers too often made scientific errors. Data also showed that Principal Greene had a weak track record hiring and retaining teachers identifying as Latino/a. While she worked on her own practice in that area with her supervisor, she needed to ensure that those teachers were on the right teams to support their retention.

Principal Greene and her HR partner then identified a series of next steps to close the gaps between the teacher teams she had and those she needed to support her teachers in leading their own learning in teams. First, Greene shared her analysis with her current teachers to see if any were interested in shifting grades or schools. Her HR partner had a roster of teachers at other schools who had been science majors and had an interest in changing schools.

And the bench was even deeper than that thanks to a partnership between the district and a local teacher education program. Through that partnership, the recruitment team and program faculty members had already been working to increase the number of graduates specializing in science education. Enhancements to the teacher hiring process also now provided principals like Greene with detailed information about each candidate's readiness to perform in different content areas from performance tasks and other sources. The superintendent added:

> You are going to ask me, "What about unions?" Union leadership helped us design these processes, and teachers are integrally involved at every step. We grew a partnership from day one. And the whole idea is to stop doing PD and staffing *to* teachers and start lifting our teachers up as professionals and giving them the support and tools they need, which is our common ground. We hit bumps, of course, but we keep coming back to that shared belief and that helps us move forward together.

As this vignette suggests, HR staff in school district central offices can be important partners for school leaders in advancing equitable teaching and learning. These staff members can streamline routine processes to ensure that principals, teachers, and others focus their time on teaching and learning. They can help principals identify which staff they need in which roles and teams to ensure teacher growth in service of those results, and they can support implementation through targeted recruitment, hiring, and retention strategies, with a central emphasis on ensuring the retention and success of teachers of color. However, HR units in most districts are not set up to support that kind of strategic partnership. What do central office HR units typically do that district leaders found ripe for transformation? Which new premises grounded their transformation efforts? What are examples of how they acted on those premises? The following subsections address these questions. Most of the examples related to how HR handled the recruitment, selection, development, and retention of teachers. In chapter 7, we discuss the implications of their efforts for other staff members, including paraprofessionals and principals.

LIMITATIONS OF LONG-STANDING WAYS OF WORKING IN HUMAN RESOURCES

Once central office transformation got underway, HR staff members in most districts, unlike their T&L counterparts, were not surprised to be in the first phase of their district's central office transformation initiative. In one district's annual stakeholder survey, school principals consistently ranked HR lowest of all central office units in terms of support for schools. One principal reported in an interview that HR's lack of responsiveness resulted in prolonged teacher vacancies, among other problems, and schools typically had to be in crisis to receive timely support. He said, facetiously, "It's crazy. Last year I was lucky because one of my teachers died [so I actually received support]." When we asked another principal to whom they turned when they needed HR support, they replied, "God. But I don't think that's the answer you were looking for."

Across districts of varying sizes—from smaller districts with two or three HR staff members to larger systems with HR departments of over 100 staff members—central office leaders identified several common problems with how HR functioned. Those limitations included large volumes of red tape and business processes that overwhelmed and sometimes confused school and central office staff personnel. In addition, HR ran largely on relationships, not on reliable processes, which led to significant inequities in services to schools. HR generally focused on basic business processes and not strategy to support equitable teaching and learning, which contributed to their ineffectiveness with recruiting, hiring, and retaining teachers of color. Leaders saw these and other limitations not as inefficiencies to solve with more training or a tightening up of their existing work but as the results of fundamental mismatches between how HR had long operated and its potential to drive equitable teaching and learning—problems requiring not tinkering but transformation.

Riddled with Red Tape

Our districts' HR directors were commonly concerned that HR processes typically involved multiple, often cumbersome steps that bogged down school principals, teachers, and HR staff themselves in time-consuming and sometimes unnecessary procedures. As one district leader explained, their HR unit had "built so many steps for every little problem." Whenever a particular problem came up, "they created a step. And so it's become a twenty-eight-step process to get a contract issued, and every month, three or more of those steps change because of a new problem." Another said, "It took twenty-one people to get some of our real basic processes accomplished." A third said that, if you are a principal or a teacher, "You have your . . . benefits person . . . compensation person . . . union person. . . . And then they have their . . . people that work under them. . . . If you're an employee, trying to navigate all that is a nightmare."

Some HR staff members explained that personnel laws and policies were often so high stakes that the various steps typically originated from important concerns with keeping schools and the district in compliance. As laws and policies changed, however, HR rarely eliminated steps, resulting in unnecessary processes whose sheer complexity increased the likelihood that someone would miss a step and make an error. In the words of one HR staff person:

> HR has traditionally been one of the front lines for enforcing compliance around union contracts, and . . . regulations. So, historically, HR managers have tended to say, "No," or "Here's the fifty-two forms you have to fill out and if you jump through all these hoops, completely to my satisfaction, then yes."

Another HR staff person explained that adding steps to processes increased their complexity and actually heightened the risk of time-consuming mistakes. She said:

> This form takes like twenty-four steps to get to me, all of which require an approver. But they [the approvers] are processing so much of this stuff that they don't always look at what they are signing and then they get to me with errors. I have to correct them and then the process starts all over again.

A school principal in a midsize district summed up these concerns:

> [HR is] always losing things. . . . You could [submit] . . . your application [for someone you wanted to hire], . . . and you'd wait and you'd call back. Not only would you not get the same person, nobody knew what you were talking about. [There was nobody] who knew where your paperwork was in the "black hole." That was the expression that we used. And it was all that duplication of effort, all that chaos, all that nonsense, all that frustration.

Adding to the time-consuming nature of HR processes, much of the HR paperwork was literally on paper, with a different staff person responsible for different forms, sometimes related to the same transaction, like processing a teacher's leave request. Principals and teachers had to download or collect the forms in person and work with various staff members to complete them. As a head of HR explained, the "dot-com revolution" seems to have "taken a sharp right turn" away from the central office, leaving HR operating procedures on paper that had been automated in other sectors.

For instance, when working with one HR team, we were approached by a staff person who thanked us for our support because her colleagues were "really struggling." She explained that principals often requested her as their HR point person because she always goes the extra mile to support them. When we asked for an example, she described how she met a principal after work the previous day to get his signature on a form. "The principals know they can count on me for that." We asked, "But why wasn't the form already available to the principal for an online signature? Did the matter really require a signature?" She replied, somewhat evasively, "They really appreciate my help."

Even in the smaller districts, routine, largely technical demands overwhelmed HR staff, leaving them little time to take a step back and reconsider their work, let alone improve it. As one HR director explained, one of the reasons why HR had "not transformed itself into a driver of human capital development and the things that a strong HR organization can do is because these transactions have basically been all they had the bandwidth to focus on." An HR director who was the only full-time HR staff person said, "I need to be able to clone myself." She went on to say that she took the HR director job after being a principal for many years specifically to improve how HR served schools, but "you get in here and just start running on the wheel [working within the systems we have] and you don't have five minutes to get off and think" about system improvements.

Leaders in some larger districts aimed to address the red tape by assigning a single point of contact within HR, sometimes called an HR generalist, to support a dedicated group of schools with all their HR needs. But the generalists also got bogged down in the red tape. One HR staff person in a district using the generalist strategy described it as follows:

> The schools and their staff don't receive callbacks from the generalists. . . . And I can see why. . . . You're [generalists] also being pulled out to go to meetings, and you're charged to deliver training sessions to those principals. . . . And [if a central office director] says, "Hey can you come . . . with me [to work on something else], you do it. So if the generalist is the primary point of contact [for schools] and they're [also] pulled out of the office a lot, well then they can't respond as quickly. So when the generalists get back [to the office], they can have anywhere from 200 to 300 emails or voicemails, which is crazy. Nobody can manage that.

Leaders were clear that the red tape had a direct impact on teaching and learning. As one described it:

> [The red tape is] . . . the brush you have to clear so you can focus on teaching and learning. If a teacher is spending her entire planning

period trying to call folks in [HR] to figure out how to get a maternity leave . . . they're not planning their lesson. And that's happening now. The principals are calling, which they often do, saying, "Can you help me with this, that, or the other firefight?" And then they aren't doing the work of teaching and learning.

Driven by Relationships, Not Reliability

In such a complex, person-dependent system, the quality of support that principals and teachers received from HR often depended on their personal relationships with HR staff members who could help them navigate HR processes. As a principal in a midsize district put it, "There was a time when there was only three or four people who really knew the job and everybody wanted to see them. . . . And if you were unlucky . . . you got one of those other people."

In a small district with ten schools and only one full-time staff person, principals described receiving varying levels of support from that person, depending on their personal relationship with her. For instance, one principal who reported high levels of satisfaction with HR said, "[The HR director] is the best. I can call her for anything. When teacher candidates come through, she knows what I am looking for and makes great suggestions." When we asked how the HR director knew what he was looking for, he said, "We've known each other for years." By contrast, two newer principals expressed concerns about her slow response time. As one said, "I know it's a small shop, but there's only ten [principals]. I think it's reasonable to expect a response within a few days."

Principals sometimes developed workarounds, strategies to avoid people they found ineffective. In midsize to large districts, those strategies included creating relationships with more effective staff members who would help them outside their formal work assignment. In the small districts, some principals relied on their principal colleagues or carried out HR tasks themselves. But workarounds typically created excessive workloads for some HR staff members and took pressure off other HR staff members to improve because others were making up for their ineffectiveness. As one HR director said, "You know the biggest curbs on change right now? Veteran principals! They know the system doesn't work, but they have made it work for them, so they don't want to see change." In the case of the smaller districts, principals risked operating out of compliance with HR rules. The HR director in one of those districts explained, "It's a little [like] anything goes out there. You can't run HR on word of mouth or what we've always done. Unless you want the state crawling all over you."

When the principals with the "right" relationships were disproportionately White or serving majority White schools, workarounds fueled racial inequities. For example, a principal identifying as a Black woman shared that, at the time, most of the new principal hires were people of color serving schools with large populations of students of color. Those principals did not yet have the relationships with HR staff members that were necessary to take advantage of workarounds, and they disproportionately struggled for basic HR support. A longtime principal of color explained that the challenge was not just the time it took to build relationships but likely implicit bias. In her words, "When I started, I was new and Black and [particular HR staff] were White. But then I wasn't new, but we were still Black and White, and there still wasn't the relationship. How is that not about race?"

Focused on Basic Business Processes, Not Strategy

District leaders recognized that, even if they cut red tape and improved staff reliability, HR units had long treated their work as transactional or procedural, with a focus on limiting risk and ensuring compliance with federal and state employment law and union contracts. As a result, they tended not to engage in deeper strategic work to support equitable teaching and learning.

For example, HR staff members typically helped principals fill individual teacher vacancies as they arose, based on basic credentials related to grade level and subject matter specializations, even though teacher success largely depends on their fit with their teacher colleagues, principal, and school community. In cases where a teacher was not performing well, HR staff members often sought their removal rather than reassignment to a school and teacher team that might be more conducive to their success and, in doing so, save resources. One central office leader explained this distinction:

> We process teachers like they are paperwork that we can shuffle and toss [away]. Teachers are our most valuable resource, but we say, "Okay, here's an opening in third grade. You are certified for elementary. Hired." Or we say, "Your performance is subpar; you're gone." Instead of "What kind of school is [this]? What's it like to work for this principal? What kind of person is likely to be successful there?" And we lose talent when one principal wants a teacher out and we process that removal instead of thinking big picture about that person and why we hired them in the first place, and can we get them to a place [a different school placement] where they will succeed and stay?

Similarly, an HR director reflected, "The in-or-out culture is a terrible culture and sends the wrong message. Not one of, 'We are going to hire you and be here for you [to support your growth].' It's sink or swim here."

In addition, leaders in some districts were concerned that, once HR identified a pool of teacher candidates basically qualified for each position, they sometimes passed an excessive number of them on to principals for them to manage. In one midsize district, a principal could receive over forty applications for each open position in the elementary grades, which created excessive workloads for principals and risked hiring the wrong person, especially by novice principals with limited experience hiring.

Many HR staff members expressed their willingness to shift their work but reported they lacked the background in teaching and learning to do so. For example, the HR director in the district with ten schools mentioned above had formerly served as an executive assistant, was promoted to director of HR because of her responsiveness to principals, and said that she received no training for the role. When we asked her how she knew what work she should be doing, she replied that she does what principals ask her to do. We asked about new principals who may not yet know what to ask her for or experienced principals who may be asking for the wrong things. She replied, "Yeah, those are tough ones."

In a typical example from the larger districts, an HR staff person described their first months on the job as "the wild west. . . . I had [an HR handbook] and the basic employee orientation. Otherwise, they showed me to my desk and the emails started coming in and you just . . . feel your way along."

HR staff members also described the limitations of not being included in the planning of T&L initiatives that had significant staffing implications. For instance, a long-standing HR staff member in a midsize district reported that districtwide improvement initiatives there were like "a clown car. There's always another one coming out. . . . And for each one, you have these schools who now need staff with background in this or that, and they act like they can snap their fingers and have them. Doesn't work like that." She went on to describe that principals would then complain about HR's lack of responsiveness when their late notice of staffing needs put them "in an impossible position."

Limited in Their Effectiveness with Recruiting, Hiring, and Retaining Teachers of Color

Leaders in the small to midsize districts reported that the problems above, as well as implicit bias throughout their HR functions, limited their effectiveness with recruiting, hiring, and retaining teachers of color. As one superintendent put it:

> Our lowest yield rates [for teacher hires] and our worst retention rates are with our teachers of color. We've got students [of color] who go years without a teacher who looks like them. We know the research on this [the problems with limited teacher diversity reflective of the school community]. We say we care about it. And then— look at the numbers. That problem starts right here [with HR].

The superintendent went on to describe how she inherited an HR department that for years had the same two recruitment team members: White women who went to job fairs and cultivated networks that resulted in mostly White job applicants. "This region is tough for diversity but not impossible. If you want different teachers, you have to start to do things differently."

Several HR directors cited red tape in their hiring process as a main contributor to their consistent loss of candidates of color across positions. As one explained:

> The competition [with other districts for candidates of color] is fierce. The more days it takes for us to move the [hiring] paperwork through, the more likely we are to lose them. And then we throw up our hands and wonder where they all went. It's mind boggling.

But he and others also identified biases in hiring criteria that systematically excluded some candidates of color. For instance, one new HR director conducted an audit of the race and ethnicity of candidates alongside the rubric they used to rate applicants. He found that several of those criteria favored certain kinds of training that White candidates tended to have more access to than candidates of color. They also detected hiring trends that suggested implicit criteria such as the tendency for hiring teams to prefer teacher candidates from two teacher education programs with majority White students.

In another district, a cross-department group of staff of color from T&L and HR convened to analyze their district's challenges with diversifying their teaching force. They started by recounting their own experiences with what they called microaggressions during hiring, including interviewers who mispronounced their names, referred to them by the wrong name, or assumed they knew other teachers of the same race in their districts. "You get so used to that," one Latinx woman reflected. But "what it says is, 'we don't care about you,'" which becomes a major contributor to teachers of color accepting offers with other districts.

In addition, those staff members reflected that, when their district did hire teachers of color, HR placed those teachers of color in schools without sufficient attention to the conditions that mattered to their retention. One provided the example of a principal with high rates of turnover of teachers of color. "And what do we do? We keep placing those teachers there because they have [the school has] low diversity [and] ignore the conditions that are creating that situation in the first place."

Similarly, an HR director in another district recounted how, for many years, exit interviews with teachers leaving the district reflected differences by race: White teachers tended to exit because of family relocation or wanting to stay home with young children, while African American teachers reported feelings of isolation that they attributed to being the only teacher of color among their immediate colleagues. He said, "These are familiar workforce dynamics for us, and we keep doing the same wrong things [like] spreading teachers of color across schools rather than placing them in ways likely to support their retention and success."

Many HR directors pointed to the teachers' union contract as a major curb on their efforts to recruit, hire, and retain teachers of color. Almost all of them noted that the contract dictated that teachers with the longest tenures had priority in choosing their placements and were relatively protected during times of reductions in teaching staff. In districts that had made recent gains in attracting teachers of color, such union rules mean that the teachers most likely to lose their placements or positions during reductions were teachers of color because those were the teachers with the shortest tenures.

One union office director explained that the retention problem also stemmed from lack of initiative by HR leaders. He said that HR departments "like to blame us" for their ineffectiveness. "They say the contract, the contract, the contract." He then showed us what he characterized as a standard provision in most teacher contracts for central offices to pursue waivers of contract terms. "The purpose of that part is just what we are talking about. To encourage change. Innovation even. But guess how many waiver requests we have gotten in my years here?" He then made the shape of a zero with his hand.

NEW PREMISES

Our district leaders all made the redesign of HR a major part of their central office transformation efforts from day one and aimed to rethink all aspects of how HR operated. As one district's annual report about HR transformation described:

> The goal of HR transformation is not simply to improve the efficiency of [long-standing] processes within . . . HR but to improve . . . effectiveness. It addresses all elements of the HR organization, including how it is structured, how people are deployed, how technology is used, how processes are designed, and how services are delivered.

Districts' strategies varied in their details but generally reflected the following new premises about what a central office's HR unit does when it supports schools in realizing equitable teaching and learning. Namely, such units eliminate, streamline, and redesign routine business processes continuously; redesign teacher recruitment and selection; and partner with principals to staff teacher teams strategically—all while driving equitable teaching and learning as their core purpose. We elaborate on each of these premises below.

Eliminate, Streamline, and Redesign Routine Business Processes Continuously to Free School and HR Staff Time to Focus on Strategic Support for Equitable Teaching and Learning

A main first phase in addressing the problems noted above involved stripping HR of its red tape by eliminating and streamlining routine business processes, starting with those that cut most into principals' and teachers' time. In addition, through what some leaders called business process redesign, staff members set current procedures aside and built fundamentally new ones that proactively supported equitable teaching and learning.

Several HR directors emphasized that this part of HR transformation was not simply about creating efficiencies but about teaching, learning, and equity. As one expressed:

> [I've worked with my staff to help them understand that] . . . we don't want to just move it [our work] to a digital process where we just upload our current forms. I want my staff asking, "How can we change our processes to reflect that teachers and principals are our primary customers? Which changes will save time, not as an

inherently good thing but a resource we need to redirect to deeper equity work?"

Another HR director explained that the main purpose of improving HR business processes had to be the improvement of equitable teaching and learning:

> We were a part of [a national network on HR redesign] which got us started. . . . But if your question is, "How do I make our work more efficient in general?" which is what it was [the focus of the network], then you are staring down an endless list. And we did that and got . . . overwhelmed. . . . They [the network facilitators] kept telling us to prioritize "pain points" [especially cumbersome processes], but everyone [in HR] had their own and it just created this competition [about] "Whose got the worst pain?" And in the end, we were spending less time on the transactional but not more on the strategic, and [we started to wonder] what's the point. So we started to ask instead, "Where are we taking the most away from [principals' and teachers'] time in classrooms? How do we make that [removing the main detractors from equitable teaching and learning] our North Star? And then, how do we do one better and directly support it [equitable teaching and learning]?"

Research on district central office HR units is thin, but it does highlight the importance of HR improving and aligning its core processes to strengthen teacher quality and diversity as drivers of equitable student learning.[1] Such efforts free HR units to take on strategic support for teaching and learning and to staff schools in ways aligned with their equitable teaching-and-learning goals.[2] Studies also suggest that, without streamlining and aligning various HR processes, other reforms are unlikely to lead to improved support for schools or teacher quality.[3]

In fact, HR directors and staff members whose units had progressed with implementation were able to demonstrate saving principals' time—time that principals could redirect toward work with teachers. For example, in one district, HR staff members estimated that, for each step that they eliminated from a process, they saved a principal approximately fifteen minutes, which added up to between two and five workdays. In a larger district, staff members could show a significant reduction in HR staff time engaged with basic business transactions that they redirected toward supporting principals with strategic staffing, as described below. The HR director in a midsize district and his counterpart in a small district estimated that their initial work in this area led to a 35 to 45 percent reduction in HR staff time spent on unnecessary business processes and the correction of errors.

In practice, HR units engaged in the elimination and streamlining of routine business processes in some similar ways. For example, one HR director first had his staff members track how much time they spent supporting principals on certain tasks and their overall task completion rates, and he helped them use those data to rank-order processes to eliminate or streamline. He also asked the staff members who were most requested by principals to identify what specifically they had been doing to save principals' time and to recommend how to make their practices standard operating procedure. Through both of those processes, he said, the culture "got transformational" because HR staff members started to see themselves as part of a system that was important for supporting equitable teaching and learning. They felt empowered to develop new strategies in service of those goals.

HR staff members in another district began the elimination and streamlining process by reflecting on their own experience and interviewing principals and school staff personnel to identify routine HR transactions that took a significant amount of time for principals and teachers to complete. They initially surfaced twenty-six processes that matched those criteria. They determined that about half of those were unnecessary (they were processes that had been developed under old state laws and union contracts) and eliminated those. The rest involved many steps, various forms, and multiple people across each process. Staff members then created streamlined versions of each process with fewer steps in an online platform. Because the platform guided users through each step with embedded instructions and examples, HR staff members and principals no longer needed to participate in trainings on the processes, and the embedded instructions reduced errors, which saved additional time for school and HR staff.

In another district, staff members from HR and the technology unit jointly developed a similar online principal- and teacher-facing platform with embedded instructions that also sent reminders to principals, teachers, and other staff members about deadlines. The HR director said, "It pops up and it says here's your . . . task list. And here's what you have to do for this month and next month. And here's links to the tools you can go to that help you do that." He explained that the system aimed to reduce school staff dependency on HR by helping them "know where to look to get the support" while also improving the timeliness of their decisions:

> We rolled out a system that . . . basically nudged them to try to make their decisions in a timely fashion . . . [and have] enough time to complete any processes. . . . And that system was actually much loved by principals, amazingly, because . . . you could have imagined they would view it as a burden to have these emails . . . saying, "Please do this," but in fact they viewed it as a very helpful organizing device. And . . . we did see an increase in timely decisions, and the reductions in frustration and errors was staggering.

Beyond eliminating and streamlining processes, HR staff members also worked on what one district leader called business process redesign—a more fundamental rethinking of core processes and how to align them with support for equitable teaching and learning. She explained that some processes were unnecessary or too long, but for others:

> [They are] just broken. . . . Spread across staff . . . and beyond repair. Those we have to toss out and begin again. . . . But it's more than that. We have so many gaps. Those are the things we could be doing but never had the time or support for. Now we ask ourselves, "What should we be out doing to support [equitable teaching and learning]? How can we build that out?" . . . And really the goal is to make that our core work.

One midsize district demonstrated an example of redesigning processes to support equitable teaching and learning. This district faced a persistent challenge with its substitute teacher fill rate; many classrooms that needed substitute teachers went without them despite the HR unit having four full-time staff members (out of about forty total) dedicated to finding and placing substitute teachers. As the HR director explained, there was "a lot of manual labor on the part of the substitute office just to process assignments. Routine stuff that didn't need that level of staffing. . . . On a good day we just got bodies into buildings." She said, "There was no tweaking this system. We had to transform it."

First, HR and Technology Services staff members worked together to automate and reduce errors in most of their processes so that, according to the director, fewer HR staff members "can spend more time having high-quality interactions with substitutes." The HR director then worked directly with staff members and various data to identify main root causes of the substitute fill rate from an equity stance. They found that the district average fill rate obscured how, in the words of one staff person, "some substitutes were not willing to go to some of our schools. . . . So we had some low-fill schools that people were just like, you know, had bad reputations or whatever else." By "whatever else," the staff person meant that those schools were in high-poverty areas serving predominantly Black or Latinx students.

HR staff members then visited those schools with principal supervisors to, according to the HR director, "actually go meet the principal and see teachers and students. And that's dramatically changed the fill rate in some of those schools" because now HR staff members "know those schools beyond rumors or reputation and why they are good communities to work in" and they "take the time to advocate for those schools" when talking to substitute teachers. Principal supervisors also began to engage their principals in reviewing their data on teacher attendance to explore strategies for reducing the need for substitute teachers in the first place.

One of the goals of eliminating, streamlining, and redesigning routine transactions was to free HR staff members and other resources for strategic support for equitable teaching and learning in schools, so those shifts invariably meant cutting of some HR staff positions and the movement of staff members to new ones. Several HR directors took care to manage staff transitions actively and respectfully as an integral part of this aspect of HR transformation. One director explained:

> We forced . . . the person who knows everything about maternity leave or benefits or compensation . . . to document how they do what they do . . . to take the knowledge of how to do these transactions [and make it visible to everyone]. Many of those processes no longer require staffing, so of course staff worry about [keeping their] jobs. . . . [So HR transformation] created some anxiety around that. . . . Most of them are also here to serve [children and schools]. We said to them, "Look, we need you to serve but in the right ways. We need you problem solving, not sitting on a pile of information [other staff members] are going nuts trying to get a hold of.

He elaborated that such conversations helped staff members understand the importance of the shifts, especially in cases of role elimination, and that training facilitated the transition of some staff members to new roles. One of those staff people corroborated the changes:

> What's evolving right now is taking this huge transactional burden off [me and my colleagues] . . . taking out the stuff that could be done more mechanically. Now we can really focus on serving schools. . . . Which is the reason I took this job in the first place. . . . And this is the first time I've been here that I have training [including] . . . a coach to help me do that.

However, some HR staff members either did not want to take on new roles, or their directors did not see them as particularly well suited for them. For example, one staff person admitted to us that she was two years away from retirement and was not interested in retraining. Perhaps not surprisingly, many other HR staff members across districts with deep expertise in the outdated transactional work were also close to retirement. Some of those people chose early retirement. In the case of the HR director in the small district discussed above, her superintendent had her handle the shrinking number of basic business processes that required staffing and hired a new HR director to engage in new strategic partnerships with principals, phasing out the old role with the former director's retirement.

Ensure That Teacher Recruitment and Selection Drive Equitable Teaching and Learning

In acting on this premise, HR units were shifting key parts of their hiring processes from their long-standing technical compliance orientation to strategies for ensuring teacher quality and diversity as main drivers of equitable teaching and learning. Their efforts reflected the research, noted in chapter 1, that shows a clear relationship between the quality and diversity of teachers and students' classroom learning, especially for historically marginalized students.

In addition, some researchers have specifically demonstrated how recruiting and selecting teachers using criteria aligned to clear standards of teaching quality may support district equitable teaching-and-learning goals.[4] More recent research suggests that, to avoid exacerbating disparities, teacher recruitment and selection should be rebuilt with race-explicit approaches at their core. The latter includes prioritizing recruitment of teachers of color, ensuring strong relationships with preservice preparation programs at minority-serving institutions, stripping hiring criteria of race-based biases that disadvantage candidates from historically marginalized groups, and training hiring managers on equitable hiring practices.[5]

When taking action on this premise, HR leaders and staff members *created a teacher profile*—a set of recruitment and selection criteria based on the district's standards for equitable teaching and learning (per chapter 2), research, and original data they collected about their teacher workforce dynamics. For example, one HR director described working with a university professor to identify research-based predictors of teacher performance along their teaching-and-learning standards and making those predictors the basis for the profile. He said that, now that they have an initial set of predictors for their hiring process, "We are looking at structured interviews, résumé analysis [based on the predictors]. . . . And then when our data system has matured . . . we ought to know over the next three years how do those teachers perform? Did our predictors hold up?" He said that building the teacher profile in that way required that they consider a range of data that they had not traditionally collected. In his words:

> [We have to move] beyond [does the candidate say they are] trying hard or being compassionate or teaching what you're supposed to teach or showing up on time or being an A student in college or coming from a top quartile or bottom decile school. . . . It's about understanding the particular constellation of quality skills and characteristics that you bring to the classroom [that supports] student learning. . . . And I think that over time we are going to start to get a good idea about what counts.

Another HR director described developing their profile, in part, by examining cases of successful teachers:

> You have to . . . think about experiences our candidates have had and knowledge bases that we haven't considered before just because the software we have always used didn't have a field for that or someone didn't think it was important. You have to go find out why did that one teacher over there have significantly higher attendance with . . . [African American and Latinx boys] who are absent four times more than their White peers. . . . Where did they do their teacher prep? What kind of mentoring [did they have]? What did their applications look like—or not look like because we didn't ask the right questions? Then that kind of information becomes standard.

Then several districts used their profile as the basis for new *recruitment* strategies. For example, those districts launched campaigns that promoted a vision of their teachers as distinctive in their commitment to equitable teaching and learning and of the district as deeply supportive of their growth and success. As one HR director explained:

> With the teacher profile, we are saying it's not enough for a candidate to be certified. . . . They need to be ready to perform on day one. . . . New teachers will be in a different place. But when we use the profile, we are saying that even they need to come in ready. Now our recruiters are more strategic about where they look for candidates. And when they go out, they are sending a message of "A [district] teacher is highly valued," which has been important to our culture building. The message is "High fliers, apply here! If you are serious about your growth and serving [historically marginalized students] . . . we want *you!*"

This quote also captures the emphasis of many HR leaders on the transformation of recruitment as a teaching tool that helps teacher candidates build their understanding of the district's expectations of them from their first encounter, and it reflects, in one HR director's words, "the culture of care" the district aimed to create for their teachers. They elaborated, "We see recruitment as the start of teacher induction in that way."

District leaders also built their recruitment teams and strategies to deepen their relationships with networks likely to draw candidates of color. For example, many districts shifted the racial makeup of their recruitment staff from largely White to African American and Latinx. Staff from one team showed us how their recruitment itinerary had previously focused on large job fairs sparsely attended by candidates of color. Through focus groups with current teachers and exit interviews with departing staff members, they learned that candidates of color were more likely to apply for jobs when recruiters met them in other, smaller settings and connected with them while they were in classes or internships for their preservice programs; in response, they enhanced their presence in those spaces.

In three districts, leaders developed so-called grow-your-own strategies to strengthen the quality and diversity of their teacher candidates. Those strategies commonly encouraged high school students and instructional assistants and other paraprofessionals to pursue teaching as a career, with a focus on people of color. They did so by offering incentives such as tuition waivers for completion of course-work toward becoming a certificated teacher and stipends and men-toring for working in the district upon receiving certification.

Staff members in several other districts also enhanced their recruitment efforts through new partnerships with teacher prepara-tion programs, with the aim of ensuring a pipeline of candidates from those programs already working toward the district's teaching-and-learning standards, again with an emphasis on candidates of color. As one HR leader described, the goal is "to get universities and our training programs to be more oriented around what we care about, which is standards-based instruction, assessment, data-driven deci-sion making, and a diverse teacher workforce."

For example, recruitment staff in one district met regularly with university faculty and district T&L staff to explore better aligning the curriculum of the university's teacher preparation program with the district's standards, in return for the district providing student teaching placements and new pathways to employment for program students. In another district, university and central office recruitment staff worked together to tap networks likely to help them increase the number of candidates and, ultimately, applicants of color. In one case, those networks included new relationships with historically Black colleges and universities in other states.

Districts also strengthened their teacher *selection processes* in ways that promised to drive equitable teaching and learning. For instance, many districts engaged in performance-based hiring that helped them move beyond candidates' basic credentials to gauge candidate readiness to grow along the district's teaching-and-learning standards. Three districts required candidates to submit video recordings of their teaching, which trained raters then scored using a rubric based on the district's teaching-and-learning stan-dards. A few others had candidates observe videos of other teachers and assess them for teaching-and-learning quality; then hiring teams used the accuracy of the candidates' assessments in their selection process.

HR staff members also scrutinized their selection processes for race-based biases and other forms of discrimination. As a result, several districts created new mandatory training in antiracist practices for teacher candidate interviewers and rooted out biases in their hiring criteria. As an example of the latter, staff members in one district explored why, on average, candidates of color routinely received lower scores on their applications than White candidates. They found that initial screening criteria favored candidates from teacher preparation programs that were majority White, and that those criteria devalued pathways that attracted more candidates of color. Subsequently, they reweighted the criteria to erase those biases.

One district also cut the red tape in their teacher selection process by enabling recruiters to offer contracts to highly competitive candidates on the spot at recruitment events. As one recruitment director explained:

> We lost top talent when we failed over and over again to turn leads into applications and then applications into hires. Some candidates you don't need a vacancy to know you want them. And in this region the pool of candidates of color and native Spanish speakers is thin. You have to be prepared to move on those [candidates] and communicate clearly that they will be valued here [in our district].

Partner with Principals to Staff Teacher Teams Strategically, with an Explicit Focus on Supporting the Retention and Success of Teachers of Color

This premise called on HR to support equitable teaching and learning by helping principals use staffing as a main lever of improvement—moving away from staffing individual vacancies reactively, as the vacancies arose, to proactively building teacher teams to foster teacher growth, performance, and retention. In the process, HR leaders and staff members were supporting the shifts in T&L discussed in chapter 2 by ensuring that teacher teams had the right complement of staff to lead their own learning.

Staffing to teacher learning teams was consistent with sociocultural learning theory's emphasis on the importance of learning in communities of practice—groups of people with the right mix of experience to grow together while engaging in authentic work in real time.[6] For example, communities of practice have members who can model new ways of working for less experienced members in ways essential to the growth of both experts and novices.[7] In addition, ensuring teachers of color are intentionally placed on teams with other teachers of color can support their retention and success when doing so breaks typical experiences of isolation, tokenism, and lack of support.[8] Districts have realized improvements in these areas by supporting principals' decision-making, including their strategic use of data and their engagement of teachers and other staff members throughout the hiring process.[9]

In acting on this premise, some districts were helping principals develop strategic staffing plans—forward-looking visions of the educators they thought they needed on each of their schools' teacher teams over the next three to five years to ensure those educators would learn well together toward the district's teaching-and-learning standards as well as the goals and strategies in their school improvement plans. In one district, a strategic staff planning protocol guided school leaders through questions such as "How many teachers who are already expert in our key goal areas do we need on each team to accelerate teacher learning in those areas?" To help school leaders answer such questions, HR staff members provided them with a growing repository of research and experience about team composition for learning.

For example, one district's research-based guidance on team composition encouraged principals of dual-language schools to include at least one native speaker of the non-English language on each team. The guidance also advised that no team have only one teacher identifying as African American without the teacher's explicit agreement or regular opportunities to collaborate with similarly identifying teachers on other teams. This district's T&L unit had already made significant investments in training teachers in inquiry-based science methods, so HR staff members encouraged schools to consider spreading teachers with that experience across teams rather than continuing to send additional teachers to that training at considerably higher cost to the district. In another district working on inclusion of students receiving special education services, guidance prompted teams to consider having a teacher expert in inclusion on each team.

Principals and HR staff members then conducted a gap analysis of the differences between their current and future teacher teams and worked with district recruiters to develop time lines and strategies for identifying teachers who fit the district's teacher profile and also met individual school needs. For instance, one high school principal said that the strategic staffing process helped her forecast that, in three years, she would need new teachers for her math and science departments. She said that in the past, she just would have "checked the box" that her needs were in those subject areas. The strategic staffing process helped her consider that her school's improvement plan had a strong emphasis on social emotional learning and that hiring math and science teachers with that experience would help ensure that the school maintained its momentum toward its goals during the staff transitions.

The gap analysis process also asked principals to consider how they could shrink the gaps themselves by moving the teachers they had. For instance, in one district, prompts in the process asked questions like, "If we could freely move the teachers we have to any teacher team, what gaps in our analysis could we address? How can I engage my teachers in a conversation about these gaps and possibilities and help them explore shifting positions?" In another district, the two supervisors of secondary school principals worked with their principals to facilitate such voluntary moves across schools, including setting aside time at their principals' meetings for principals to share their staffing plans and discuss current personnel.

In these and other districts, HR staff members also collected and analyzed data about each school's staffing dynamics and used those data to advise principals about hiring decisions. For instance, those staff members explored such questions as, "Which teachers does this principal tend not to retain, and how can we limit the placement of teachers with that profile with that principal? What is this principal's leadership style, and which teachers tend to thrive under that leadership style? What relationship is there, if any, between where a teacher completed their preservice preparation and teacher growth and retention at each school?"

As more information became available about each school's staffing dynamics and teacher candidates (through performance-based hiring and other mechanisms), those in recruitment and hiring roles began to provide principals with strategically screened pools of candidates for each position that required a new hire. For example, one HR staff member showed us how, in the past, she would have about twenty-five candidates who met basic eligibility criteria for a given opening and just pass those files on to principals. But the new data and relationships with principals meant they could narrow the pool significantly for each position and discuss with each principal deeper issues of fit, such as "Of the candidates with undergraduate majors in mathematics, which are also strong in reading as demonstrated on the performance tasks? Which candidates are already demonstrating leadership potential and could assume the department chair vacancy you anticipate in four to five years?" One longtime recruiter described the changes:

> I love my job now. This is how I always thought it was supposed to be. It's like a real partnership with schools where we know what they need—what's the vision, where are the real needs, and I know the principals pretty well and what to look for [in teacher candidates to match with principals], but what's really cool—well, two things. First, we have this information years ahead, so I really get to stop and think and get out ahead. . . . Recruitment is about relationships, and we sometimes need time [to build the right relationships]. . . . Principals trust us more. . . . Everyone is happier. It's very cool.

What HR leaders did *not* do is seek changes in their teachers' union contract as a precursor to these reforms. Instead, they aimed to build principal and teacher support for the new staffing processes within current contract terms. One HR director said:

The PLC and planning time is already there [set up for teachers and guaranteed in the teachers' union contract]. What we have done is create conditions where that can be more powerful learning time and supports for teacher learning should they [teacher teams] decide to go there.

When explaining how HR had been able to move teachers within and between schools, one HR director said simply, "We asked." He elaborated that the success of strategic staffing depended on teachers collaborating on the creation of the staffing models and, through that process, coming to see moves as growth opportunities. He added that he hoped the various changes in HR would "create a new culture where teachers are here to serve the district, not this one school or principal." Our teachers need to be more like "utility players," a sports reference to describe teachers who can fit and are willing to serve in multiple roles. Other HR directors reported that new district marketing strategies aimed to attract applicants who understood their job as serving the district as a whole, not a single school or position.

SUMMARY

These new premises anchored a fundamental rethinking of how central office HR units operate when they serve as main supports for equitable teaching and learning in schools. For principals like Robin Greene, the differences were like night and day. She and her colleagues experienced less red tape and improved functioning of long-standing processes like routine requests for teacher leaves. HR began to provide new support for helping her school realize its instructional vision and to recruit, select, develop, and retain teachers of color. Those efforts reinforced T&L's emphasis on growing teacher teams, as discussed in chapter 2, which further supported teacher growth and success.

For principals like Robin Greene to take advantage of these new supports, however, they needed to deepen their understanding of how to use staffing strategically and otherwise support equitable teaching and learning throughout their schools. Principals' growth in those and other areas of instructional leadership was significantly bolstered by shifts in principal supervision from compliance, operations, and evaluation to dedicated support for principals' instructional leadership growth. Those shifts in principal supervision are the focus of chapter 4.

CHAPTER 4

From Principal Supervision to Support

PRINCIPAL CHRISTINA BELL hung up the phone after talking to a parent and asked her office manager to do her best to handle all other calls for the remainder of the morning. She laughed to herself, remembering how only last year she felt like she walked around with a sign around her neck that read: "Complain to me. The principal is always in!" Last year, she spent only a small fraction of her time in classrooms and otherwise working on teacher development. With the help of her principal supervisor, Jan Jackson, she turned her calendar upside down. Now she spends 60 percent of her time each week on activities such as observing the quality of classroom teaching, talking with teachers one-on-one and in small groups about the observation data and next steps, and supporting her team of teacher leaders in their leadership of teacher professional learning communities (PLCs). She said that she hopes to increase her time on these tasks to 75 percent within the next year, adding:

> For years I have been putting out fires—responding to parents, finding out where is that facilities request I put in months ago. . . . And other things like, why was I spending ninety minutes a day or more on cafeteria and recess? Jackson asked me some hard questions in my

one-on-ones like, "Why are you doing that? Who else can be on the yard to free you up for other things you need to do to move instruction in this school?" Which really bothered me. That's not why I became a principal. I always thought I'd be the principal who was all about my teachers. But then the phones ring and the fires start. One thing leads to another, and you are in your office dealing with this one student all day or whatever else.

When we asked her to describe her relationship with her supervisor, Principal Bell said:

> The old supervisors were more like bosses. You escalated things to them. They made sure you were checking all the right boxes. If I couldn't get something done in central office, sometimes they could help. And they did their observations for the evaluation, but the less they were in your building, the better. With Jackson, it's exactly *not* that. It's more of a partnership. She understands our students. She keeps us focused on instruction, instruction, and instruction. She keeps me focused on the classrooms and the kids, which is her focus too. I look forward to her visits. We are in it together.

To support her instructional focus, Principal Bell and Principal Supervisor Jackson kicked off the year with a self-assessment of Bell's capacity to lead for improved instruction. As part of that assessment, they reviewed various evidence, which Bell had assembled herself, that she thought indicated her instructional leadership abilities. The evidence included her teacher professional development plans, teacher evaluation ratings, student assessments, and Jackson's observations of Bell's leadership practice. When discussing the data, Jackson pointed out that Bell had rated 90 percent of her teachers at the top of the teacher rating scale. But student performance data revealed that only half of her students were reading at grade level and that student achievement in mathematics was below the statewide average and not keeping pace with growth across the state. Observations of Bell's leadership practice suggested limited knowledge of strong mathematics instruction and that teacher professional development (PD) tended not to focus there. Jackson's observations of mathematics teaching suggested students were generally compliant but not learning at deep levels and, of particular concern to Jackson, Bell had not picked up on those dynamics in her own observations or discussions with teachers about student work.

Bell then developed a learning plan for herself that focused on sharpening her skills at supporting mathematics instruction as well as two other priority areas for the year. The plan emphasized steps that Bell would take on her own during her regular day, including inviting another principal and a teacher leader to observe mathematics instruction with her. She also added a conference on ambitious mathematics instruction where she could attend sessions on principal leadership. Principal Supervisor Jackson then suggested ways she could support Bell's learning plan by checking in periodically on her evidence of progress and attending the conference with her, since leadership of math instruction was a growth area for her as well.

Principal Bell was also able to add several monthly principal meetings to her learning plan thanks to Jackson's early intentional planning. Jackson anticipated that a common focus for her principals this year would be their improved leadership of mathematics instruction, and her review of her principals' learning plans so far that year confirmed that trend. In response, she planned to dedicate a series of twice monthly principals' meetings to their leadership growth in that area. She was already working with staff members from the central office Teaching and Learning (T&L) unit to develop those sessions around specific leadership growth targets.

We asked Principal Supervisor Jackson how she managed such intensive focus on her principals' growth as instructional leaders. Jackson explained that she sometimes has to "discipline the system," adding:

> The rest of the system is in the process of their own change, but we aren't there yet. So I have to be able to say "Sorry, can't come to that meeting, be on that task force, because I'm focused on my principals," or, "No, you can't come to my principals' meetings to talk about that one program—if its informational, put it in the weekly principals' admin packet." And then, when I'm working with principals, I always remember that my job is to support them. Support doesn't look like me letting other demands get in the way of the work. It's not coming in here and giving orders and then checking back next month. It's also not me doing their work for them. My job is to help principals learn

what they need to be great instructional leaders and create conditions for their success as instructional leaders. That's it.

This vignette illustrates the experience of a principal in a district working to transform its long-standing approach to principal supervision.[1] Those in principal supervisory roles had various titles, including assistant superintendent; school director; and, in smaller districts, superintendent and had traditionally focused on principal evaluation, compliance, and operations. District leaders aimed to shut down those traditional roles and replace them with one relentlessly focused on helping principals grow as instructional leaders. Which limitations with traditional forms of principal supervision did district leaders seek to address as part of central office transformation? What new premises were reflected in the forms of principal supervision we associate with improved support for principals' growth as instructional leaders? What are examples of how principal supervisors and *their* supervisors realized those premises in practice? We answer these questions in this chapter.

LIMITATIONS OF TRADITIONAL APPROACHES TO PRINCIPAL SUPPORT FOR INSTRUCTIONAL LEADERSHIP

As we noted in chapter 1, leaders across our districts were concerned that realizing equitable teaching and learning required new forms of principal leadership, sometimes called "instructional leadership." But the principalship historically had not focused on instructional leadership, and principals had not received much support for their growth as instructional leaders. District leaders saw principals' supervisors as key influences on principals and believed that when principal supervisors focused mainly on evaluation, compliance, and operations, they did not reinforce and, in some cases interfered with, principals' instructional leadership.[2]

Principalship Insufficiently Focused on Instructional Leadership

This insufficient focus was evident in various ways, including principals' job descriptions, which led to the hiring of principals with limited understanding of and experience with instructional leadership. In the words of one Human Resources (HR) director:

> To look at the old job description—and I used to do a lot of principal hiring—you would have thought, like many [candidates] did, that the instructional elements were on equal footing as the operational and managerial. . . . And you get what you search for . . . so many [principals] who have been in the seat for a long time understand the job as largely that [operational and managerial rather than mainly instructional].

A chief academic officer similarly commented:

> In just the span of my career, the work of teachers has changed . . . and become so much more demanding around [ensuring students'] understanding and subject matter expertise and what principals do has really lagged behind. . . . We can't have that. An instructional focus starts at the top. . . . And the research is really bearing that out. . . . We can't have principals in their office all day . . . and we can't be pulling them out of their buildings.

Leaders also highlighted how principals' evaluations reinforced a diffuse focus for that role, with instructional leadership added on as one among many elements. Several leaders explained that, when you take the old managerial focus of the role and, in one leader's words, say "instructional leadership too," you are communicating "now, with everything else, now improve instruction. . . . And to look at the [principal] evaluation [standards], how clean your building is is just as important as are your Black and Brown students meeting or exceeding standard." She added, "We realized we were rewarding principals through the evaluation process for things out of step with who we were trying to become as an equity-driven system."

Another leader elaborated on this observation, explaining that instructional leadership reflected a profound shift in the nature of what principals do, but their district simply added it to the list of what principals were evaluated on "without rethinking the core." He said that, given the multiple demands on the principalship, that lack of prioritization meant principals tended to focus their time on what they were comfortable with or did well, which, especially for most of their long-standing building leaders, was not instructional leadership.

Weak Support for Principals' Growth as Instructional Leaders

District leaders were also concerned that professional learning opportunities for principals were limited and generally did not help principals grow as instructional leaders. To illustrate, at the outset of central office transformation in one district, we talked with a T&L director of science education who highlighted that she did not offer PD sessions specifically for principals, but she encouraged principals to attend the sessions she provided to teachers. When we asked her how a principal learns their role in supporting the then-new science standards, she replied that principals needed to know what they were seeing in classrooms when they observed. We asked how PD helps them know what to look for. She showed us a tool designed for teachers to help them plan classroom tasks and pedagogical moves, and suggested principals could use that document, which ran close to fifty pages. As the chief academic officer in this district put it, "It's unmanageable [for principals]."

Sessions designed specifically for principals typically focused on operational matters. For instance, in one district, regular meetings cast as principal PD took place in a central office training room and covered various largely operational topics such as new purchasing software and the employee assistance program. In one meeting, principals completed budget reports. One principal summed up these PD sessions as "85 percent management and 15 percent instructional."

The few sessions that addressed instructional matters tended to involve pulling principals out of their schools to receive information rather than providing opportunities to improve their instructional leadership practice. For example, at one meeting, district math specialists told principals about a new math assessment and rules to follow during administration, but they provided no time for principals to consider, for example, how they might support their teachers in using the assessment to improve the quality of their instruction.

In addition, principals' access to PD opportunities sometimes depended on their school's standardized achievement tests scores, not their demonstrated capacity to engage in instructional leadership. That approach sometimes led to mismatches between the PD that principals needed and what they had available to them or what they were required to attend because student test scores are, at best, a weak proxy for principals' capacity, especially in districts that have committed to staffing their low-scoring schools with strong instructional leaders. For example, in one district, the principals of chronically low-scoring schools were required to attend PD sessions on various instructional topics. However, one of those principals had been placed in one of those schools because of her instructional leadership strengths. This principal reported that the sessions were largely a waste of her time, saying, "I really just need to get to work here [at this school]."

Principal Supervisors Focused Mainly on Compliance, Operations, and Evaluation, Not Principals' Instructional Leadership

In all our districts, principal supervision had long focused on compliance and operational matters and the evaluation of principals. District leaders viewed that traditional form of principal supervision as nonstrategic and out of step with their emphasis on the principalship as instructional leadership. They noted that it did not contribute to particularly strong support in the areas of operations or compliance either.

To illustrate the nonstrategic nature of the traditional role, we asked a team of six principal supervisors in a midsize district simply, "What is your job?" We filled seven pages of chart paper with comments such as help with staffing, graffiti removal, getting coaches for teachers, high school steering committee, monitoring implementation of the superintendent's priorities, parent questions, principal hiring, principal evaluation, sounding board, email responder, budget, and conflict mediator. When we asked how they accomplished all these tasks, one summed up the group's approach by saying, "You follow the smoke," meaning that issues that generated the highest levels of frustration by principals usually gained their attention.

Some principal supervisors suggested that, when they engaged in operational and compliance work with principals, they saved principals' time tracking down requests for building repairs or approvals related to teacher and staff hiring and that principals appreciated the help. However, those principal supervisors could not provide any specific evidence of time savings. Many principals we interviewed expressed frustration with their supervisors' operational and compliance focus. As one principal reported, he had always wanted a principal supervisor who could be "more of a thought partner" with him in his growth as an instructional leader but historically that was "not the reality."

Some district leaders were also concerned that principal supervisors' approach to principal evaluation missed opportunities to provide principals with meaningful trusted feedback that could improve their instructional leadership practice. For instance, in most of our districts, principal supervisors started the school year by having their principals set goals as prescribed by the state evaluation process. All the goals we reviewed addressed areas of growth for students and teachers and were otherwise related to school improvement, not targets focused to how principals wanted to develop their own practice in service of those results. Principal supervisors then conducted the required number of school visits, sometimes observing classrooms without principals present, and issued evaluation scores at the end of the year with minimal comments related to principals' instructional leadership. One chief of schools reflected, "When the evaluation is pushing paper, you get paperwork, not progress."

NEW PREMISES

At the heart of their central office transformation efforts, district leaders called for the elimination of traditional principal supervision that emphasized compliance, operations, and evaluation. Instead, principal supervisors were to dedicate their time to working with principals one-on-one and in principal learning communities to support principals' growth as instructional leaders. Some principal supervisors did focus their time in that way and demonstrated improved results in terms of their principals' enhanced understanding of instructional leadership, an increase in time they spent on instructional leadership, and the ability to engage in progressively more challenging instructional leadership tasks.[3]

We distilled from our data the premises that principal supervisors support principals' growth as instructional leaders when they operate with a clear conception of their role as a dedicated support for principals' growth as instructional leaders, support principals to lead their own learning as instructional leaders, supplement that leadership with one-on-one coaching and facilitation of principal learning communities from a teaching-and-learning stance, and receive similar support for their growth from their own supervisor.

Operate with a Clear Conception of Their Role as a Dedicated Support for Principals' Growth as Instructional Leaders

All our districts recast the principal supervisor role as a main dedicated support for principals' growth as instructional leaders. As one district leader described, if you are a principal supervisor in this district now:

> Your role is . . . to develop principal capacity to function as instructional leaders in their schools. Which means that you need to . . . give feedback, and coach people. . . . You need to know what it is that principals [need to grow their instructional practice]. You need to be in school to see how principals are doing these things.

This premise reflects research on adult learning discussed in chapter 2 on the importance of learners having a clear image or definition of the practice they aim to develop to anchor their learning.[4] When communities share and reinforce the value of those definitions, learners may experience increased motivation to learn and help learners identify themselves as being on a trajectory toward mastery, which is also essential to their progress.[5]

In practice, district leaders engaged various staff members in developing or adopting a definition of the principalship as instructional leadership, and principal supervision as a central support for it. For example, one district started that process by convening a team of principals and central office leaders to examine their district's definition of high-quality teaching with questions such as, "What kinds of principal leadership supports that kind of teaching?" and "What kind of principal supervision could reinforce that principal leadership?" As a leader of that process described:

> We sat down as a group . . . [and] we needed to define . . . "What does that [principals acting instructionally focused] mean?" It's observing classrooms. It's meeting with teachers to give them feedback. It's planning professional development. It's preparing for anything related to schoolwide goals and data analysis. All of that is instructionally focused.

He elaborated that then they asked, "If a principal supervisor were supporting principals in engaging in those instructional activities at a high level, what would they be doing?" The group then built their responses into a new job description for principal supervisors.

As this example suggests, districts typically did not tinker with their long-standing principal supervisor job description but sought to rebuild the job from the ground up with support for principals' instructional leadership at the core. Given the significant shift in the role, many districts had their current principal supervisors reapply for their job. As one chief academic officer explained, "Many of them [the current supervisors] have been in the role for years and were promoted for their proficiency with . . . [matters other than instruction]." She said that having the current principal supervisors reapply for the positions sends "a clear message . . . [that] . . . this is a new day."

District leaders also reinforced the importance of principal supervisors operating as a dedicated support for principals' growth as instructional leaders by publicly and proactively protecting principal supervisors' time to do so. For example, two districts created "blackout days" where central office leaders and staff members were not supposed to pull principal supervisors away from principal support. In the words of a principal supervisor from one of these districts:

> We had blackout days, right, and the blackout days were equivalent to one and a half days a week. And the blackout means that you don't pull principals, you don't pull [principal supervisors] . . . because people are in schools working.

He added that to reinforce that focus:

> [We] asked for that time to be increased and it was increased to two and a half [blackout days per week], and basically our position was it's a very poor commentary if this is our core business and we are only having blackout for less than half of the time [in the work week]. And so [the deputy] was like, "You're absolutely right. Two and a half days."

The chief academic officer in another district protected principal supervisors' time by requiring other central office staff members who wanted their time to make the request directly to her. She explained that her actions were partly practical because she would help principal supervisors manage those requests, but they were also symbolic: they sent a message that the reason why someone needs a principal supervisors' time has to be so important that they are willing to take some of her time to get it.

Principal supervisors across our districts who we associated with the positive results noted above took action on this premise themselves by protecting their own time to support principals' growth as instructional leaders. In the words of one principal supervisor:

> There is no way that you can ensure that children are learning, the teachers are teaching, and that principals are monitoring the quality of that unless you are in those schools. . . . You have to be in those schools 50 to 75 percent of your time, and you have to have the courage to say, "I can't serve on that committee, can't go to that meeting, can't do that right now. Sorry. Tied up in a school doing my business."

Another principal supervisor similarly described:

> Last year, I got completely awash in that logistical kind of side-tracking stuff. And so we as [principal supervisors] made a commitment to twenty-four hours in schools focused on instruction every week. And so what I'm doing is, I'm starting to ignore the noninstructional stuff . . . and I don't feel bad about it because I'm really getting feedback, too, from the principals that our time in the schools is truly making a difference for the instructional focus and what they're doing for instruction.

Support Principals to Lead Their Own Learning as Instructional Leaders

This premise meant that principal supervisors fostered principals' leadership of their own learning throughout their day as their main strategy for supporting principals' growth as instructional leaders. Their approach reflected the sociocultural learning research discussed in chapter 2 about the importance of agency to learners' ability to deepen their engagement in challenging practices. Through leading their own learning, learners develop self-regulating behaviors that help them make sense of new practices, without which their behavior tends not to change in meaningful ways.[6] Such self-regulating behaviors prompt learners to continue to practice and seek out help with the new ways of working, even when their mentors or others are not present.[7] Conversely, when learners approach their learning passively, they tend to perform tasks perfunctorily, without deepening their understanding of what they are doing and why in ways that are essential to their realizing meaningful and lasting changes in their daily practice.[8]

Principal supervisors helped principals lead their own learning in part by supporting them in conducting *systematic self-assessments* of their instructional leadership and using those assessments to develop and implement explicit *learning plans* with principals as main drivers. For example, one principal supervisor started the school year with each principal examining evidence of his or her leadership along each of the district's formal standards for principals' instructional leadership. The principal and supervisor then used those self-assessments to identify strengths and areas for growth and to develop specific plans that the principals would execute to lead their own learning. To supplement the support that principals could access on their own, the two then added a role for the principal supervisor in the learning plan, including prescheduled meetings throughout the year for the principal and supervisor to check on their progress.

Another principal supervisor met with each of his principals at the start of the year to discuss what the evaluation would say if it were conducted at that time. The principal supervisor explained that completing a draft of the evaluation at the start of the year rather than at the end meant that he could dedicate his time on the principals' growth instead of evaluation because the principals already knew their scores unless they improved over the year. His principals then chose two or three aspects of their leadership as their main emphases for the year, identified concrete next steps they would take to support their own growth, and planned to collect evidence of their progress. Then the end-of-year meetings focused on how well principals had led their own learning and any changes in evaluation results.

Principal supervisors also *modeled for principals how to lead their own learning.* In one instance, a principal supervisor explained to her principals that her own main area for growth that year was to stop spending most of her time directly coaching principals and to focus more on helping principals lead their own learning. Her learning plan included readings she would do with her principals on adult learning and documenting her one-on-one meetings with principals so she could reflect on ways her practice in those meetings demonstrated progress.

Another principal supervisor routinely concluded his visits with principals by identifying the specific steps his principals committed to take before his next visit as well as what he himself would do to grow in his own practice as a principal supervisor. A principal supervisor, who characterized himself as having a steep learning curve when it came to knowledge of high-quality instruction, regularly shared with principals during meetings that he was "learning too" and asked them to identify aspects of their leadership on which he could provide feedback while also learning from their often more advanced knowledge.

Principal supervisors also acted on this premise by helping principals *identify and access resources* to support their own growth. In one example, a principal supervisor had a principal who struggled to focus on his own learning, mostly because he was overwhelmed by his school's multiple challenges and unsure where to start—either with the school's improvement efforts or his own growth as an instructional leader. The principal supervisor assembled a team of central office staff members to help, explaining, "The first week of September we did a . . . blitz site visit and spent about two and a half hours in there, going into classrooms looking for evidence of teaching and learning, [and then we] gave the principal some feedback."

Some principal supervisors also connected their principals to each other as learning resources. For instance, one encouraged a principal to visit a neighboring school rather than travel across the country for expensive training to deepen his understanding of instructional leadership, specifically in literacy. Another intentionally grouped principals during her learning community meetings with them so they could access each other's expertise while engaging in particular tasks. In the words of one supervisor, "I'm like a matchmaker. I love helping my principals get to know each other that way."

Supplement Principals' Leadership of Their Own Learning with One-on-One Coaching and Facilitation of Principal Learning Communities from a Teaching-and-Learning Stance

This premise called on principal supervisors to teach rather than tell principals how to grow as instructional leaders and to use moves that help learners deepen their understanding of what new practices entail and how and why to engage in those practices and learn alongside principals in the process. A teaching-and-learning approach is consistent with research on apprenticeship relationships that support learners in deepening their engagement in progressively more challenging practices.[9] In high-quality apprenticeships, mentors engage in specific practices, including:

- Modeling: Demonstrating new work practices with metacognitive strategies, that is, explicit explanations of what they are modeling and why.
- Talk moves: Using language and dialogue to help learners make sense of how and why to engage in new practices.
- Differentiation: Tailoring assistance to each learner, often with an emphasis on amplifying strengths to address weaker areas and using evidence to personalize the assistance.
- Brokering: Bridging learners to new ideas and resources to advance their learning and buffering to protect learners from learning distractions.
- Recognizing all learners as learning resources: Creating opportunities for each learner, no matter how novice, to (1) identify themselves as a resource for others' learning and on a trajectory toward mastery and (2) see others as learning resources for themselves.

Principal supervisors who acted in ways consistent with this premise consistently engaged in these moves when working with principals one-on-one and when facilitating principal learning community meetings. With regard to *modeling*, one principal supervisor explained that some principals were "stumped" by how to improve teaching quality and many "need to see a model in action" to understand how to lead for such results. Another emphasized the importance of metacognition during modeling, saying, "If I'm going to have any impact at all on these schools, I have to teach them—and teach them *why* we're doing what we're doing and what makes a difference." This principal supervisor elaborated that unless the principals understood the underlying rationale for certain practices, they were more likely to perceive their principal supervisors as directive and evaluative rather than as supportive, and therefore resist them.

In practice, we observed a principal supervisor working with a principal who was a novice when it came to identifying high-quality instruction. Prior to a classroom visit, the principal supervisor confirmed with the principal that she would be modeling how to observe students working in small groups to understand the rigor of their task and the students' understanding of what they were doing and why. During the classroom visits, the principal supervisor stayed physically close to the principal and narrated what she was seeing in the classroom and the extent to which she thought it fit the district's standards related to task rigor and understanding, which is an example of modeling thinking. Just after the observation, the principal reflected on the experience aloud and in writing and planned to practice what he learned before his supervisor's next visit.

In another instance, at a principals' learning community meeting at a high school, principals were practicing using data about student talk in classrooms to determine if students were deepening their understanding of particular concepts. The principal supervisor framed the activity with metacognitive comments about why capturing data about student talk provided important evidence of the quality of classroom instruction. She engaged the principals in a brief discussion of strategies for documenting student talk, most of which involved sitting alongside students while they worked and taking low-inference notes. As the classroom visits began, a group of five principals entered one English class where students were working in small groups to discuss a common text. The principals stood at the perimeter of the room where the closest student group was hard to hear and otherwise did not use the strategies for observation that they had just identified.

When the principal supervisor entered the room, first she joined the principals and made various metacognitive comments about the limitations of standing on the periphery. She modeled ways of thinking by asking rhetorical questions such as, "Which student group will I sit with first and why would that one be a good one to start with?" and "Which strategy that we discussed for joining a group might make sense now?" She then walked directly to a table of students and called her principals closer to observe while she listened to the students, asked the students questions, and took notes. After repeating the process with another student group, the principal supervisor convened the principals in the hall to debrief. She asked the principals to recount how she conducted herself in the classroom and the pros and cons of her choices. After taking a few minutes to plan their approach, the principals visited the next classroom, with the principal supervisor taking notes on the principals' efforts for later discussion.

The positive examples of modeling just described feature the use of *talk moves* to foster learning in the form of metacognitive comments and discussion strategies. We also observed principals using talk moves in other situations. For instance, one principal supervisor described how, at a school with low student achievement test scores, she consistently saw unambitious teaching in classrooms but high scores on that principal's ratings of teachers in the district teacher evaluation system. This principal supervisor worked with the principal to organize and analyze the test score, observation, and evaluation data and to ask probing questions across the data. He explained:

> Every one of their teachers got 100 percent on their performance evaluations. They only have about 57 percent of their kids meeting or exceeding the state standards. A third of their kids didn't pass [the state test]. When every one of their teachers got 100 percent on their performance evaluation I said, "Who's 100 percent? . . . How does everybody get 100 percent?" [The principal said], "You have forced me to really understand this and take a look at it." Because what incentives do teachers have to improve if they're already a 95 and they don't get outcomes with kids? Why should they change their behavior?

Also for example, after a series of classroom observations at a principals' meeting, a principal supervisor started the whole-group discussion by asking principals what they saw related to the focus of that particular observation, which was student engagement. Principals initially responded with general comments about the classroom, such as "There's too much stuff on the board." One principal said that he thought the objective of the lesson was unclear because he asked some of the students what it was and they didn't know. The principal supervisor challenged the principals to sharpen their answers, prompting them with comments and questions such as: "What difference does it make how much stuff is on the board to how the teacher is actually teaching? Is it possible the students do know what the objective is but you asked them in a way that confused them? How does each of your ideas indicate something about the quality of student engagement specifically?" The principal supervisor then asked if principals saw any evidence related to particular grade-level standards. The principals all replied quickly that they did not. The principal supervisor asked, "What's your evidence?" and pressed the principals to "show me" and "convince me" that those teachers may not be teaching to the standard.

Some principal supervisors also *differentiated* their engagement with each principal based on evidence of each principal's capacity for instructional leadership in different settings in ways important to principals' instructional leadership growth. As one principal supervisor described, "different" meant working in a range of areas depending on principals' abilities and learning plans:

> It may be about sitting with their professional development team, listening to what they're trying to put together, and then asking questions to help them through that. It could be in terms of looking at classes—an initiative that the school may have and they want to see how the instruction is going, or it could be because they want a different lens on a teacher that they feel is not performing up to par and they just want my input on that. It could be a parent meeting that they're having to explain the data and how to look at the data, or things like strategies like how to read with your children or building vocabulary—activities that they can do at home. It could be around having conversations with some principals that may be stressed and overwhelmed and talking crazy, like "I'm quitting."

One principal explained the importance of differentiation and her principal supervisor's efforts in this area:

[There are] . . . principals who have less experience than I do. They're in their first year or their second year and I'm, even now with four years, in a different place than where they are. So I think that they [the principal supervisors] all understand that and I think it directly impacts the way that they work with us . . . we're not all necessarily asking for the same thing all the time. . . . It's pretty analogous to having a class full of heterogeneous students where people need very, very different things.

During meetings, we frequently observed principal supervisors differentiate by building on principals' strengths and areas for growth based on evidence of their instructional leadership, not their schools' test scores. For instance, many principal supervisors conducted their principals' meetings at rotating school sites where they positioned the host principal as a mentor for the visitors in an area of strength for the host. In that format, the principals who were more novice in that area had opportunities to benefit from seeing new practices in action, and the host principal was also pushed to grow while leading colleagues' learning. Principal supervisors also developed protocols for various meeting activities with tasks and questions in order of progressive difficulty to help principals at all levels access the activities while also supporting them in reaching for the next level.

In one-on-one settings, principal supervisors *bridged* or connected principals to resources to support their instructional leadership growth, often along the goals in their learning plans, as noted above. During principals' meetings, principal supervisors bridged to other central office staff members who could support principals' growth as instructional leaders. For example, a principal supervisor had a math coach from the central office attend a series of principals' meetings to help principals understand the implications of the new math curriculum for their instructional leadership practice. The principal supervisor explained that, even though she herself was familiar with the new curriculum, the coach brought important expertise into the group. Importantly, she worked with the coach in advance to ensure that the activities did not focus on the curriculum in general but on principals' leadership in the new curricular context.

When bridging in these ways, principal supervisors actively worked with the outside guests to ensure that their participation proceeded from a teaching-and-learning stance. For instance, two central office staffers asked a principal supervisor if they could attend a principals' meeting to discuss the district's new writing assessments. The principal supervisor told them that if they wanted to deliver information to principals, they should put that information in writing for her to distribute electronically. Otherwise, they had to work with her in advance of the meeting to connect the session to the ongoing learning plan for the meetings and to facilitate the meeting in ways that supported the principals' learning. The principal supervisor then met with them over several hours to work out their lesson plan.

At the resulting principals' meeting, the two central office staff members began their segment by sharing learning goals they used to anchor the session and how the session fit within the broader scope and sequence for the meetings. Then they asked the principals to orient themselves to the work ahead by reviewing the new writing assessment rubric, reflecting on where they thought their school fell on the rubric, and noting evidence they would explore throughout the session to check their ratings. The central office staffers then shared brief highlights of how the assessments reflected the new state standards. After they made each point, they gave the principals small- and large-group opportunities to talk through what they were hearing and reassess their initial ratings. Throughout the meeting, the principal supervisor actively mediated the participation of the central office staff members with metacognitive comments at key points to help principals further connect what they were hearing with their own leadership practice.

Principal supervisors also worked to protect or *buffer* their principals from interruptions to their instructional leadership focus. One principal supervisor described his approach by saying, "We take away those distractors. Then they [principals] don't have those time-consuming things that stop them from really focusing in on instruction." In the words of another, "I think that the core job description of being an instructional leader to the principals has to be protected and it has to be respected . . . it takes fighting our bosses sometimes."

In practice, a principal supervisor "exempted" her school from different assessments in an effort to help the principal focus their time on instructional improvement. The principal elaborated, "All the schools are supposed to do all of these 10,000 assessments throughout the year, which are completely invalid for [my school given our demographics]. [My principal supervisor] exempted us and talked [the Assessment department] through that." One principal summed up such work, "I say, . . . 'Do I really have to do this? This is stupid.' And [my principal supervisor] is like, 'Oh you're right, that is stupid; I'll get back to you.'"

Buffering in principals' meetings involved limiting or denying requests from their central office colleagues to present information to principals or to use meeting time for matters other than their instructional leadership. One principal supervisor described that he "worked hard" to keep informational and compliance issues to a short period at the end of each meeting; otherwise, they "take on a life of their own and take over the meetings." Another said that "for the compliance stuff, I put 90-plus percent of those expectations in writing. At the end of all my meeting agendas I say, 'Here are upcoming key dates. Pay attention. . . . Don't make my conversation be about compliance or operations stuff. Take care of this stuff.'"

We also observed principal supervisors *recognize each principal as a learning resource* for their peers. For instance, during a meeting, a principal asked his principal supervisor what level of detail to include when developing meaningful instructional goals. Instead of giving a specific answer, the principal supervisor called on other principals, whom he knew had been working on the same issue and asked them to share strategies.

As noted above, when selecting host school sites for their principal meetings, principal supervisors often focused each visit on an area of strength for the host principal, positioned the host as a main leader of group learning during the visit, and rotated the principals' meeting through every school in the group to reinforce that every principal member had something to contribute. During one meeting, a principal supervisor was observing several classrooms with a subgroup of his principals. Outside one of the classrooms, the principals discussed how the host principal, a fifteen-year veteran in that role, was clearly struggling to work with his teachers on the quality of their classroom instruction. They shared examples of extremely low-quality instruction they saw in the classrooms and wondered if the principal was capable of leading for better instruction. One asked the others if they should even be observing at that principal's school. The principal supervisor validated their observations, complimenting them on their use of evidence to support their claims. He then pointed out that this principal has strengths as an instructional leader, particularly in the area of knowing his students, and elaborated, "A student came in one morning to [the principal's] office and the first thing he said was, 'Good morning. Are you hungry?'" The principal supervisor went on to explain that, in this instance and in other ways, the principal demonstrated the importance of understanding the out-of-school conditions his students faced and addressing them as part of his instructional leadership. The principal supervisor said, "That's the level that he knows his kids" and explained that good instructional leaders continuously seek to understand the root causes of each student's school performance, even those outside the classroom.

Receive Support for Their Growth from Their Own Supervisor from a Teaching-and-Learning Approach

This premise meant that the supervisors of principal supervisors (SPSs) helped them lead their own learning and coached them using the moves noted above. Accordingly, SPSs' actions in this regard were also consistent with the research that we cited earlier on assistance relationships and communities of practice, suggesting a correlation between those actions by SPSs and principal supervisors' growth as learning supports for principals. Our own data corroborated that association because principal supervisors who grew in taking a teaching-and-learning stance tended to work with SPSs whose practice reflected this premise.[10]

In acting on this premise, some SPSs supported principal supervisors to *lead their own learning* in ways that were important to their growth. For instance, one SPS administered an end-of-year survey to solicit principals' detailed feedback on their supervisors and led the supervisors in reflecting together on their survey results. The SPS used a protocol that asked the principal supervisors to work in pairs to interpret what they thought their own results meant about their practice and their relationship with their principals, identify growth areas they wanted to target for themselves in the next year, and formulate specific steps they would take to succeed with their growth goals.

In several other districts, SPSs also had principal supervisors develop or adopt standards defining their new roles and use a professional growth planning process to self-assess against the standards and create intentional learning plans. In one district, the SPS had principal supervisors include her observations of their practice in their learning plans and met with them regularly to discuss their evidence of progress.

SPSs also *modeled* how to engage in principal supervision from a teaching-and-learning stance. In one typical meeting, a principal supervisor asked for his SPS's advice about how to address a series of parent complaints that a principal had asked the principal supervisor to handle. The SPS modeled thinking by sharing that, when those situations come up, he asks himself questions such as, "Will taking on this complaint help the principal engage in instructional leadership?" Through dialogue with his SPS, the principal supervisor sorted the complaints into (1) those to turn back to the principal (a form of buffering herself), (2) those to handle personally (a form of buffering the principal), and (3) those that other central office leaders could address (a form of bridging the principals to additional resources to support their instructional focus).

SPSs also *buffered* principal supervisors from distractions to keep their focus on principals' growth as instructional leaders. For instance, the blackout days noted earlier were a main buffering strategy initiated by several SPSs as was the one SPS's requirement that all central office requests for principal supervisors' time come to her first. In another district, every single principal supervisor reported that any time they brought a challenging issue to the attention of their SPS, the SPS either provided information that was needed to expedite the issue or handled the issue themselves, which increased the time they spent working with school principals on their instructional leadership. Another SPS remarked, "I know I make a special effort when [principal supervisors] call me. . . . I try to make sure they get what they need as quickly as they can because the bottom line is providing service to schools. That's it. That's it."

SUMMARY

Leaders in our districts were clear that traditional principal supervision did not align with their emphasis on principals' growth to lead for equitable teaching and learning nor did it improve compliance or operations. The new premises emphasized principal supervisors' central focus on principals' growth as instructional leaders and helping principals lead their own learning toward those results, supplementing that leadership with one-on-one coaching and facilitation of principal learning communities from a teaching-and-learning stance, and receiving similar support from their own supervisor.

Principal supervisors still faced persistent threats to their focus and stance from other central office units that had come to rely on principal supervisors to handle various compliance and operational matters for them. The ability of principal supervisors like Jan Jackson in the chapter-opening vignette to engage in their new roles depended on aligned shifts in other central office units, especially in relation to the efficiency and capacity with which operational units went about their work. We discuss those changes in chapter 5.

CHAPTER 5

From Operations to Opportunity

MIDDLE SCHOOL PRINCIPAL KENNY FABROA met driver Aleta Perry at the door of her school bus as the last student headed into the building. Inspired by videos of teachers who had special greetings for their students, the students on Perry's bus route each had their own "handshake"—a fist or elbow bump, a pose with arms crossed and a smile, or a wave—when getting off the bus. Principal Fabroa handed Perry a coffee from the faculty lounge. Hers was the last bus to arrive, so he knew something slowed her down. Fabroa also knew her coffee choice. "Light cream," he said with a smile and then, "What do I need to know?" Perry shared about the sixth grader who was upset because he forgot his lunch and the two eighth graders who seemed extra tired and fell asleep.

In the cafeteria at 11:30, the student who forgot their lunch was personally greeted by lunchroom staff and grabbed a meal and a pen. As part of the school's emphasis on writing, English language arts (ELA) teachers collaborated with lunchroom staff members to integrate writing throughout the lunch periods. This week, students were asked to assume the role of food critic and write a brief review of their experience at lunch using featured words like "atmosphere" and "presentation."

Because it was Thursday, the entire school transitioned to their environment groups at 2 p.m. This new program, planned through a collaboration between science and health teachers and leaders of the custodians' union, aimed to build students' environmental stewardship by having them work in teams to inspect and clean parts of the school building throughout the year. That week, the three groups assigned to the schoolyard worked through an inspection checklist. As they collected trash, they recorded what they found. At the end of the month, they discussed their data and strategies to improve schoolyard cleanliness. Principal Fabroa reflected:

> In this school, everyone matters to our instructional mission. Everyone. And every minute of every day is a learning opportunity, and if you are an adult working in our school, you have to be a part of our community advancing that mission. When I was an AP [assistant principal] in another district, we didn't have this. I mean I dealt with custodians and food service all the time but not in a good way and definitely not related to teaching and learning.

He said that, in that district, the operational systems had been so broken that he used to take care of many tasks himself:

> I kept a can of paint under my desk to deal with graffiti removal because those requests just went down the black hole of the district. If you had a good custodian, you were lucky. And if that guy got sick, you didn't wear your good shoes to work because, even though you double-checked all the paperwork and sent it in early, help was not on the way, which only got in the way of the instructional work.

The head of operations in Principal Fabroa's current district explained the difference:

> On one level we tightened up our systems. Made it simple to request support. But then, we recultured our staff. We said there is no "operational side" of the house anymore, which is what everyone liked to call anything not under the assistant superintendent for Teaching and Learning. We invested in them because, at the end of the day, they know their work best and how to improve it. Now everyone has a scorecard where they know the expectations and what they need to do to meet them, including ask for help themselves, which they also get credit for. It's not some gotcha thing but a way to focus and celebrate our work.

A principal like Kenny takes it to the next step. He invited all his support staff—custodians, food service, bus drivers—to send reps to his leadership team meetings. The invitation alone really lit a fire. They are part of the school's discussions from day one. You want to host this event? Well, they are there to ask the questions. What kind of space do you need? Food? Would transportation help parents attend, and no we can't use the buses like that, but maybe we could. And the drivers can go find out, or they know the routes and who is where and can suggest other strategies. And our staff are ready for that. To be that kind of strategic partner.

This chapter-opening vignette illustrates that operational functions of school district central offices—including facilities, nutrition services, and transportation—matter to equitable teaching and learning. When they do not function well, they take principals' and teachers' time away from instruction. Even more important, those functions could work in direct service of those results. However, leaders and staff members of those units historically sat on what the leader above referred to as the "operational side" of the district, often with little connection to discussions about teaching-and-learning improvement, let alone opportunities to engage in it and training and other support to do so. In our study districts, what more specifically were leaders' concerns about the ways their operational units had long functioned? Which new premises did their transformation efforts reflect? What are examples of how those premises played out in practice? This chapter takes up those questions.

LIMITATIONS OF LONG-STANDING WAYS OF WORKING IN OPERATIONS

Across our districts, leaders were concerned with parts of their central office that handled operational matters. These units typically reported to their own assistant superintendent or chief and included transportation, buildings and grounds/facilities, purchasing/procurement, and nutrition services.[1] As we elaborate in this section, leaders' concerns about these units echoed many of those they identified with Human Resources (HR), including inefficiencies and inequitable workarounds. Leaders also saw the potential of these operational units to support equitable teaching and learning more directly, but that those units lacked learning opportunities and other resources to help their staff do so.

Riddled with Inefficiencies and Inequitable Workarounds

District leaders as well as principals identified inefficiencies with the long-standing work of many operational units as taking time and other resources away from instructional matters and, in some cases, creating extreme frustration. As one district leader explained:

> Every time a principal has to spend more than a few minutes trying to get that graffiti removed or the carpenters to fix those shelves . . . that's time spent away from the instructional core. . . . And you get the message that you and your school aren't important . . . or valued here, which distracts [you] and wears you down too.

A school principal shared an example of this dynamic related to a request to have a hallway painted:

> There's an online repair system, work order program, we put them all in, hit the button. We did that three or four times. My office manager made some phone calls [and said] . . . "Come on guys, I need you to paint, I need you to paint, I need you to paint." And it doesn't happen.

One principal described their experience with the district purchasing department in even sharper terms, saying:

> If I send something [a request] . . . and I miss a line, like I forget to write something on a line, instead of calling me and saying, "Hey, let me write down what you are missing. Just tell me what to say." It sits on somebody's desk, and we don't hear for weeks. Then, when we inquire, they'll say, "Oh, you did it wrong, so we're going to send it back. We're going to send the whole thing back and go through the whole process again." And I'm like, "All you had to do was call me for this one line." That frequently happens.

Some principals, often those with longer tenures with the district, were able to work around the inefficiencies by identifying and developing relationships with individuals who were more reliable. As one described:

I think it's easier for me and people like myself who have been here for a while. . . . I've learned over the years who is in charge of what. And although it changes daily, weekly, monthly, I can usually figure it out pretty quickly who to go to. . . . And then who will actually help.

In the words of another, "They all suck . . . just a bunch of road-blocks because no one problem-solves. . . . So, we have to figure creative ways to get around it. . . . And you learn who says yes [and you go directly to them]."

One director of Teaching and Learning (T&L) explained these dynamics arose in part because heightened accountability policies increased principals' urgency to get their operational needs met "by any means possible" so they could focus on instruction. She said, "In a moment of need, . . . [a principal] turns to whoever can get the information [for them, but that] is one of the problems in terms of how central offices work right now."

But she and other leaders were also concerned that some work-arounds reflected the kinds of inequities that we shared in chapter 3. As one chief operations officer put it, "A lot of these teams are good-old-boy networks . . . male and White. And it gets pretty insular." She went on to share the results of a time study that showed slower response rates by many operational units for principals of color and schools serving majority students of color and low-income students compared to their White counterparts and schools in White and higher-income neighborhoods. She elaborated, "You could say that those schools have more needs. But that's a whole other level of inequities around which buildings have been most neglected. Which playgrounds need upgrading. . . . Which bus routes have the most absences [among drivers]."

Disconnected and Distracting from Equitable Teaching and Learning

Many district leaders recognized the potential of their operational units to support equitable teaching and learning proactively but that in reality, those units were generally disconnected from it. Some operations staff members saw and felt this disconnection as well.

For example, one district's T&L unit held a week of professional development during August in one of their large high school buildings. Despite the sessions occurring routinely every year, the T&L organizers generally did not consult with facilities staff, which sometimes resulted in buildings not being clean or otherwise ready for the events. A director in facilities said, "We are an afterthought. [I told the head of T&L], 'Invite us to the planning meeting. Get us in on the ground floor of the planning.' But we never get the call, and then it's a scramble to backfill [and] help and everyone's just deflated."

District leaders also described ways that operational staff members detracted from the school experience of students, especially those living in low-income circumstances. Pointing to a then high-profile case in the national news, a head of operations said, "That could be us." The case involved cafeteria staff shaming students who owed money on their meal accounts. She said, "Every single adult interacting with a student shapes the learning [environment]. . . . What happens in the lunchroom or during passing period—if a custodian makes eye contact . . . gives you a smile. Safety and learning happen in those moments, [that's where we say] you are valued here."

Not Hired or Supported to Advance Equitable Teaching and Learning

District leaders also expressed that the results above were predictable. As one said, "You get what you hire and train for." She elaborated that operational units selected staff members for their technical skills and appropriate certifications, not for skills specific to working in support of the instructional mission of a school system, and they received little to no training in that area. One facilities director described that, in her district, "a carpenter is just a carpenter." She elaborated that the district has always hired facilities staff for their qualifications in a discrete trade with little consideration of what is and could be different about being a carpenter in school buildings. She added:

It's not just about efficiencies, like can you get those shelves up quickly so a principal doesn't have to spend time [tracking down the request]. It's about being a strategic partner to the principal. What is the vision for students here? How can the physical environment reflect that? But we don't hire staff for that skill set to have those conversations. That's not how we have helped them understand their jobs.

A chief operations officer made a similar point about staff across operational units, explaining that those staff members tend to come to their jobs with little understanding of the contexts of schools, minimal training beyond their singular functions, and sometimes little training at all. "And then our systems are antiquated, and we hire staff to run those systems."

Most district leaders described the workplace training for operations staff as focused on the technical aspects of their job, not strategy to support equitable teaching and learning in schools. As one put it, "School starts when those [school bus] doors open" but we have not treated drivers like they are part of the school day or provided sufficient training for them to be a more contributing part. They go to schools every day and some of them "have never been invited inside."

Some leaders recognized the racial nature of that lack of investment. In the words of one head of operations, most of the operational staff are:

classified people who . . . are parents and live in the community. . . . [In some areas] they are the Black and Brown faces in the schools. Because most of the teachers and administrators are White . . . the people, the adults in the school that look like the kids are the classified staff. And they've been treated pretty badly in this district. And they've had no training. The kids are smart. They know what message we are sending to them.

She elaborated that "true equity work" starts with "how you treat your people, and by that I mean each and every employee. On that count I give us a C-."

Her counterpart in another district similarly expressed that, for years, they had advanced community engagement strategies as part of their equity efforts, but they never looked internally at their own staff members, who were community members themselves. She said:

> If we trained and developed the classified staff and made them true partners—that's the highest level of parent engagement work we can do. Because these folks are the parents . . . they live in the community. But we have not seen or valued those staff [members] that way. It's a profound contradiction.

NEW PREMISES

As we discussed in chapter 1, an overarching premise of central office transformation is that everyone matters when it comes to realizing equitable teaching and learning. District leaders were acting on that premise by working with staff members in operational units—mainly facilities, transportation, and nutrition services—to transform their work to realize those results. Their efforts reflected the premises that an operational unit contributes to equitable teaching and learning when it ensures that routine services maximize school time and other resources for instruction, engages with school principals and others as a strategic instructional partner, and supports the leadership and growth of operational staff members.

Ensure Routine Services Maximize School Time and Other Resources for Instruction

This premise meant that leaders of operational units were pursuing major changes in their long-standing core work processes to minimize the amount of time that principals, teachers, and others spent on operational matters. As one deputy superintendent described this focus:

> The message [to operational staff members] is we want a transparent level of support, meaning in a perfect world, there would be no distractions whatsoever. If you're an educator in the classroom, I don't want you to have any distractions. . . . And from an

operations standpoint, we are doing everything that we possibly can to support the schools in a timely and efficient manner. That we're not wasting our money. That as many of the resources as possible go into the school or supporting schools. That we operate at the most minimal level that we can to be efficient. Which means really analyzing and understanding our needs and that we understand from our operations side that our only reason we're existing is to ensure that our schools do well.

As another central office leader put it:

When an employee goes to work [in a school], a lot of things run through [their] mind. If we assist those employees, [we] . . . relieve them of a lot of their pressure so that they can go back into the schools and concentrate on the main focus of the students. We're here for the students. So if we can assist . . . [school-based employees] and accommodate them as much as we can to relieve that stress and that tension, they can devote their time to teaching the kids.

Districts' own data about the performance of their operational units suggested significant improvements in time savings for teachers and principals, which they translated into dollars that could be reinvested in teaching and learning. For example, time studies in two districts revealed that principals initially recovered half a day, on average, each week thanks to the improved functioning of operations, and those time savings later increased to a full day; in a school board report, the head of operations shared what those days amounted to in terms of principals' salaries, which they cast as funding now available for instructional matters. A leader in another district explained how in prior years several operational units had posted "huge deficits" that they had to pay for out of their district's total general fund dollars, "which means those are dollars that are not going to the classroom." The improvements in those units "took care of all that."

In acting on this premise, leaders in several districts engaged operational staff members in creating *performance management systems*, including performance targets, routine examinations of performance data, and specific plans to improve. For instance, a team of custodial staff members and their union leaders developed various "standards of service," such as ensuring principals spent less time on operational matters. They then analyzed their long-standing work processes to identify specific areas for improvement, data that would show progress, time lines with benchmarks, and incentives for achieving them. Throughout the year, they shared status updates in a regular report on the district's progress with central office transformation.

In another district, operational leaders similarly collected data and facilitated challenging conversations with their teams about their performance and next steps. One leader described that, for some operations staff members:

> Those meetings are . . . very, very uncomfortable. . . . [One person] told me literally, . . . "No one has ever said that to me" [i.e., that I need to do a better job]. I said, "You're living down here in a fog, buddy. Everybody thinks that you guys suck! I'm here to tell you! . . . So let's go about doing some of the things that we can do to help change that perception because that perception really is everyone else's reality except yours. . . . What planet are you living on that you think everything's going well?"
>
> Once they saw the data, they couldn't unsee it. . . . And it really got interesting when they started collecting their own [data] about strategies other districts were using or even ideas from other industries. . . . We even held a design competition where staff had to work together to invent innovative solutions, and they came up with prizes for like "most out-of-the-box thinking" and "most likely to succeed."

Leaders in these and other districts also acted on this premise by creating specialized, time-limited groups, which we call *operational improvement teams*, to support rapid and sustainable improvements in routine operational processes. As one chief operations officer explained, this strategy aimed to create "quick wins," improved processes that would make a demonstrable difference in staff performance and that could be developed quickly with the help of staff members experienced in business process redesign who reported directly to the cabinet. A leader in another district said:

> So [the operational improvement team] was developed to . . . take the burden off [operational unit staff members] . . . to figure out how to reinvent their work and to bring in the expertise that redesign work requires. . . . That kind of outside help is important . . . [when] the challenge isn't just how do you make existing work better. But . . . when you have major gaps—services schools need but we have not historically provided . . . that takes a special skill set. The [operational improvement team members] are highly skilled at going in and tightening things up but also seeing the unmet needs. . . . And then helping [unit staff members] develop that kind of mind-set themselves and take that mind-set forward.

For instance, members of one district's operational improvement team worked across operational units to help staff members identify limitations of their current work order and purchasing systems and specific modifications that would improve system functioning. Team members then engaged cabinet leaders to ensure targeted investments in new software and other infrastructure to support implementation. In another district, team members identified so-called home-run projects, lines of largely operational work within the central office that, if improved or created, promised to dramatically increase principals' time spent on teaching and learning. At the time of our study, those projects included the development of a new payroll system and work order processing software related to custodial services projects.

Operational improvement teams also typically worked between units to create aligned infrastructure changes. In the words of one team director:

> HR needs shifts in [the] technology [unit, which] needs shifts in budget. They all need to get it to the [school] board for approvals [of certain budget allocations infrastructure improvements]. We realized we had to, at least in the near term, assign people with know-how across the organization to go in like a SWOT team and coordinate all the improvements.

A team leader described how they worked across units with the following example:

> So [we] had this meeting [with one unit] and . . . say, "Well, why can't this get done?" [Staff members responded], "Well, so-and-so's . . . [a staff person in purchasing is not doing a good job with their part]. So at that next meeting, I had the purchasing guy there at the table. [I asked], "Well, why can't this be done?" [They said], "It's technology." So, the next meeting we brought technology in. "It's HR," [they said]. So we brought HR. Then it's other people in finance. So eventually we had everybody at the table—everybody. Because I said, "Whoever you point the finger to, you will have to point it to their face."

In addition, staff members on those specialized teams recognized that part of the challenge with the way that many operation units functioned was a lack of reliable infrastructure within schools for handling the school side of operational matters, and team members worked in schools to build it. According to one district's annual report, that year the operational improvement team's school support included training principals and school front office staff members on use of the new online substitute teacher management system, receiving and creating requisitions, and time management, as well as the rearrangement of the physical space in the front office to support staff effectiveness.

As an illustration, a school principal shared how they had been struggling with new software for various work processes and called on the operational support team for training. The team member assessed the situation and identified the root of the principal's struggle in the workflow in his front office. She then trained the office manager on the software and worked with her to develop a new system for handling deliveries and visitors and her own interactions with operational staff members.

Working within schools also helped team members align their central office improvement work with school-level realities. One team member explained, "We got [the new budget and work order management software] and it's state of the art. But then you sit with [a school office manager who doesn't use it] and see the problem. . . . Part training, part experience, part software needs adjustments to better meet schools where they are." A team member in another district described how they had been collaborating with school office managers to create operations manuals for various work processes. They then worked with different central office units to build those instructions into the new online platforms as an integral part. In the team member's words, "Now they really just need to find the 'on' switch" because the user interface walks them through the necessary steps.

Engage with School Principals and Others as a Strategic Instructional Partner

Transformation meant not just doing long-standing work faster and better but also engaging in new strategic partnerships with school principals and others as direct support for equitable teaching and learning. As one head of operations explained, the shift is:

> to take problem situations and turn them into strategic opportunities. So a principal contacts us frustrated with limitations of the physical space. The first thing we say is, "No, that's against code, but what are your goals? What are other creative ways of accomplishing what you want? Let's see if there's another way that it can be done." And then next time, what if we are already thinking about the relationship between the facility and learning and make suggestions proactively . . . if we are involved at that level. So we are getting our staff to work like that and for principals to think like that.

Districts' own data supported the importance of this premise. For instance, in one district that conducted an extensive annual districtwide satisfaction survey, custodial services achieved 23 percent growth in principal satisfaction with custodians' service quality and demonstrated commitment to problem-solving. A similar survey in another district showed a gain of 44 percent in principals' perceptions that nutrition services staff members were "reliable strategic partners."

In practice, the nutrition services director in that district coached her staff members on how to take a strategic approach to principals' requests that they had previously denied—to use those requests as jumping-off points for exploring what principals were trying to accomplish and alternative pathways to those goals. She said, "Now when we still have to say 'no' we say 'no, but . . .'" She provided examples of principals wanting to serve meals family style, in take-out packages for pickup so absent students wouldn't go hungry, or at rotating food stations reflective of the food of different cultures—all of which in some way violated laws related to use of federal funding for school meals. Her staff members first talked with school staff about alternatives such as using other funds that provided more flexibility. They also took time to explain the limitations related to federal funding for meals and health codes, framing them as their shared constraints, and invited school staff members to partner with them on identifying other approaches. She summed up this new strategic stance, explaining that it helps principals and other school staff members:

> [They] step back. . . . Let go of the one solution and think through what are they trying to accomplish. . . . What are other ways to get there, like not using federal dollars? How can your PTA [parent teacher association] help? Yeah, we could seek a waiver and . . . [in the meantime], are there other ways to meet your goals?

The head of operations in another district facilitated a series of meetings between directors in nutrition services and T&L staff as well school principals and teachers to consider ways to align students' experience during meals and otherwise in the cafeteria space with instructional goals. He elaborated, "[The directors of T&L] had just come from a conference on extended learning time and were really inspired to think differently. . . . It opened up possibilities . . . [about] partnerships across the district."

This leader then shared one product of those meetings—new materials to support conversations between teachers and cafeteria staff members about how to encourage reading and writing at lunch and make eating spaces language-rich environments. One set of materials for elementary schools included small dry-erase boards that were color-coded by grade level and that provided guidance on how teachers could work with cafeteria staff members on integrating vocabulary words throughout the cafeteria. The head of operations also created incentives for cafeteria staff members to support physical education and health teachers by participating in lessons related to nutrition and other aspects of wellness. He said that classroom teachers could always teach those lessons on their own, but it creates a richer learning experience if cafeteria staff members participate as additional knowledgeable adults and consider how they can support learning outside the classroom.

Examples related to custodians reflected a similar emphasis on new partnerships to enrich student learning. For instance, one district's head of operations encouraged school principals to include their custodians in their leadership team meetings or meet with them regularly one-on-one to talk about their involvement in the school's instructional vision. As the head of the custodians' union described:

> It was humanizing. It helped our membership understand you don't work for a building; you work for *students*. What can you do today to support their day? It can be as simple as a smile or saying hello [student name] or asking how their day is going. . . . [We always had staff members] who worked like that. The change is [now] it's everyone. . . . [It's] our expectation . . . [it's] what it means to work here. And it goes both ways. . . . Students have more positive interactions in schools, and our members feel valued.

The environmental stewardship initiative featured in the chapter-opening vignette was based on an example of a collaboration between science and health educators in T&L and leaders from the custodians' union. Together, they developed a program to support students in taking responsibility for the cleanliness and safety of their school campuses while learning about leadership, the environment, and public health.

In this and other districts, new relationships between the central office and the local leadership of the teamsters' union likewise began to expand the role of bus drivers as a teaching-and-learning partner. The example of Aleta Perry in the chapter-opening vignette was inspired by drivers in one district who participated in a new program to help them engage with each student in developmentally and culturally appropriate ways and another around attendance. As one leader explained the latter, first-period teachers still take attendance, but now the bus drivers do too, which means the front office knows even before first period or when students line up in the schoolyard who may be missing. She elaborated:

> Then the office managers start calling [guardians of students who seem to be absent], which has been another resource that's gone underutilized. . . . And what's evolved is now the drivers know the students not just by face but by name and more. . . . And they . . . see themselves as having a role in each student's day. . . . You get on the bus and now you get, "Hey, [student name]. We missed you yesterday." Or "Hey, man, good to see you." How can that not start your day right and get you to think twice [about missing school]?

In another district, bus drivers received new incentives and training not just to provide transportation but also to serve as chaperones on visits to museums, aquariums, and historical sites.

In one rural district where many students spent considerable time on buses, the head of operations provided incentives to drivers and teachers to collaborate around creating a culture on school buses that supported students' homework completion, including quiet periods and drivers celebrating completed work with students as they exited. And in another rural district, the director of career and technical education worked with their district's bus contractor to help students explore jobs in transportation and automotive repair. He described how students in one introductory class worked with the contractor's managers to analyze and advise on bus routes, shadowed drivers during their safety inspections, and assisted with vehicle repairs.

Invest in the Leadership and Growth of Operational Staff
Members to Serve as Strategic Supports to Schools

To help realize the shifts described above, district leaders engaged operations staff members as main drivers of the transformation of their own work and invested in their growth to lead the change. As one deputy superintendent emphasized:

> [You] . . . get to an improved performance culture . . . when staff build that culture [and when you] humanize the change process so, through building the new culture, staff come to live it. Anything else is the old "management says," and look how little that has gotten us.

A union leader similarly explained why it is important to invest in staff leadership and growth, saying, "A higher performance standard is meaningless unless people have a pathway to success. Without it, it's a setup."

Leaders' efforts in this area reflected organizational management research on the importance of tapping and cultivating knowledge and leadership at every level of an organization to organizational performance.[2] Scholarship on expansive learning processes highlights staff members' "transformative agency" as a vital resource for the invention of new work practices, especially those that address long-standing and seemingly intractable workplace problems. Transformative agency includes participants' individual and collective beliefs that they can exercise control over the problems they are encountering and successfully work with others to address them. As participants develop transformative agency, they start to identify themselves as essential and able leaders of fundamental, systemic change and use their voice to advance the change process.[3]

In acting on the first part of this premise around cultivating staff leadership, a nutrition services director participated alongside her staff members in a series of work sessions over several years to design new principal-centered strategies for their work. She recounted how, in the first year, she persuaded her staff members to focus on the goals she chose. She said staff members bought into the work that year, but the buy-in was "next level" in the second year, when she stepped back and let staff members pick their focus and lead more of the process themselves.

As noted above, in several districts, custodians developed their own metrics as well as learning plans and met consistently to discuss performance data and improvements. The head of one custodians' union confirmed that his members were "in on the ground floor" of these efforts; they "selected the training program . . . [and] developed the pilot as well as the success criteria for the learning plans." Another union leader corroborated, "We've all heard the talk, 'all employees are valued here' [and] 'everyone matters to school success.' The difference now is we are at the table."

District leaders also invested in the growth of their operational staff to engage in such leadership. As noted above, the performance management systems in several districts provided structures, support, and additional resources for staff growth. In discussing learning plans with employees, the chief operations officer in one district identified staff interest in pursuing formal higher education. In response, district leaders created a partnership program with a local community college to facilitate staff members earning their associate degrees. In her words, "[A community college] is right across the street but may as well have been in another state [given how inaccessible operations staff thought it was]. We created a win-win where we invest in you pursuing your degree and you apply your learning here in the district."

One operations director created opportunities for what she called "just-in-time learning." She elaborated:

> Twice a week we have stand-up meetings where our teams literally stand up from their desks and huddle to share one success story and one challenge for feedback. . . . We collect the stories and circulate them in our newsletter. We recognize employees every month, which is part celebration, part saying, "Here's what we value. Here's a model you can aspire to."

Another director of operations showed us menus of training options for operational staff members. The choices included the usual opportunities around workplace safety but also new sessions on leading effective teams, conferences typically attended by health educators, and districtwide professional development for teachers and principals that operations staff members were now invited to attend. Staff members were also encouraged to develop learning opportunities themselves for inclusion on the menus.

We observed one session where a union leader and a T&L staff member facilitated a design competition for facilities staff. Staff members received several examples of common school events and classroom activities, and the challenge to develop advice for principals and teachers on how to maximize their use of physical space in each context. As the facilities director described:

> When they approached me about it [running sessions like these], I thought it was just a fun idea. A way for staff to get to know each other [for] . . . team building. But then you go there and you see they take it very seriously. Old-timers push new employees to think outside the box. . . . And every now and then, you see the light bulb go off, "Oh, I am not here just to take orders."

SUMMARY

As part of central office transformation, district leaders aimed to ensure that every district resource worked in service of equitable teaching and learning. That emphasis meant breaking down traditional distinctions between academic and operational services and investing in operational staff. Those investments focused on enhancing the efficiency and effectiveness of long-standing operational work and building staff capacity to support teaching and learning. As a result, principals like Kenny Fabroa were able to save time and other resources handling operational issues and engage with operational staff members, including custodians, bus drivers, and nutrition services workers, as teaching-and-learning partners.

Realizing such shifts depended on various new collaborations between directors of operations, various unions, T&L, and HR to rethink traditional job descriptions and performance criteria and to ensure new training and other benefits for employees. We found that particular ways of working on the superintendents' executive team or cabinet provided vital support for these new relationships. We elaborate on these developments in chapter 6.

CHAPTER 6

From Telling to Teaching and Learning on the Superintendent's Cabinet

SUPERINTENDENT INTERN LAMAR JONES set his laptop down close to Superintendent Cameron Stow's usual seat in the central office training room, although he knew it didn't matter. Stow's cabinet members never sat for long. In fact, after the superintendent made a few welcoming and framing remarks about the meeting's main activities, they were up and working throughout the room.

The cabinet members knew the drill well. Early in their central office transformation for equity initiative, they had collaborated on an overall theory of action or logic map detailing how and why the central office needed to shift to support equitable teaching and learning in schools. Then they focused their meetings on building unit-specific theories of action to guide their staff members' learning and work. They were convening now for their quarterly analysis of alignment across staff and functions.

Cabinet members rotated from one to the next of four stations in the meeting room. Each station had different parts of the overall district theory of action on a large poster. Their task was to comment with specific data points where leaders had seen the necessary alignment across the parts during the last quarter. For example, one station showed the theory of action about Teaching and Learning (T&L) and how their shift to focus on teacher learning teams in their approach to teacher professional development depended on Human Resources (HR) building its strategic staffing function. At that station, the head of T&L left several brief narrative examples she had prepared in advance to illustrate how HR's staffing efforts were sending a consistently aligned message about the centrality of teacher teams. She also added a description of one school where alignment was especially evident in practice as well as districtwide data that showed T&L and HR had met their quarterly benchmarks for deeper implementation across the district.

The next station added facilities to the picture. There, both the head of facilities and T&L had added examples of improved responsiveness by custodial and grounds staff. The facilities director also noted several instances where operations staff members were still not being included in key discussions about instructional planning at certain schools.

Then cabinet members conducted a gallery walk of the information at each station with a protocol that asked reflective questions including: "Where do I see results to celebrate? What clarifying questions do I have about the information added to each station? Which areas may benefit from discussion today?" For the remainder of the three-hour meeting, they reviewed their responses and identified concrete next steps to address before their next cabinet meeting.

Jones took careful notes. He was a principal supervisor in another district, but he was observing Superintendent Stow's cabinet meetings as part of his internship for his superintendent certification. After the meeting, he would use his observations to prepare a status update for the superintendent's advisory board of philanthropic and public agency partners that convened three times annually for such updates and to provide advice and other support. Jones also helped cabinet members develop learning sessions for their staff members related to any next steps from the cabinet meeting. And he drove forty miles each way several times a week to do it. He explained:

Most superintendent interns do their internships with their own superintendents, but that wasn't going to work for me. I don't want to be like the superintendents I've had. I want to be the superintendent *I wish* I had. . . . Dr. Stow really pushes my thinking about how I want to lead. . . . How I need to be able to create a strategic team driving equity throughout the organization.

In Superintendent Stow's words, "Culture change starts at the top. If you want your people doing the right work and collaborating to support that work, your people need to see your [executive] team walking that talk." She knew from her conversations with central office staff members during her interview process that these staff members had experienced little of that. She said:

They knew [the previous superintendents] had a vision, but they could barely tell you what it was. Forget about showing the alignment of their work. . . . So much competition. I could tell when they were talking to me they were on wash, rinse, and repeat.

By that, she meant that staff members had experienced their previous superintendents and other cabinet leaders asking for their input on the district's direction, but that input was rarely used. Stow elaborated that she tried to change that dynamic from day one, saying:

The superintendent's playbook says, "Just listen and learn for at least the first ninety days." My message was, "We don't have a day to waste. Not for the students who've been furthest from educational justice." Any good candidate has already spent time listening during the superintendent hiring process. So I said to everyone as I met with them the first time during that process, "We are now talking. I am hearing you. We will continue to do that, and we also need to move the work forward. You already know some things that need to get done. Let's make the first ninety days about real staff engagement in developing our shared vision and action steps."

To support that orientation, she brought new staff into the district to serve on her cabinet and elevated some longtime staff people with demonstrated experience bucking the status quo to advance equity. She reflected, "But after a few months, you would have thought they had worked here for years—not in a good way." That is, despite Superintendent Stow's emphasis on their leading central office transformation, her leadership team tended to fall back into old cabinet patterns of using meetings to report on informational items with little discussion or reacting to crises. She added:

> And then they all are drowning in [school] board requests and community complaints, snow days, and what that one bus driver did. And then those bad habits saturate the system. Everywhere in the organization, staff [members] are drowning in work because we don't work smart. And we sit in meeting after meeting for the sake of meeting.

Stow realized that her team needed particular support and time to lead central office transformation, and those investments in her cabinet have significantly paid off. She explained:

> I pulled them all together, and we said, "Okay, let's imagine a world where we [the cabinet] don't meet. And each of us is leading our departments around strategy. What do we need to work on together to advance that work as our core purpose?" Then we said, "How can that be the core work we do in these meetings and throughout the system?"
>
> It took time. It took letting a lot of old work go. But once they did, they saw the ceiling didn't cave in; no one missed that memo or actually needed so many of us at that one community event, and they started to trust the process. And then we built new cabinet routines around our theory of action and alignment, which made our meetings about the real work. They started to see their colleagues as key to their success. That it's okay to be vulnerable and seek feedback and support. Then all of that permeates how they work with their staff. And that's where true alignment happens, and alignment to the right things.

This chapter-opening vignette underscores that central office transformation for equity depends on shifts in the core work of senior central office leaders who often sit on the superintendent's cabinet or executive team. Without those shifts, staff at all levels can remain bogged down in long-standing work and unproductive meetings, their leadership and expertise for change and improvement may go underutilized, and the complex work of transformation likely will not advance. What kind of cabinet leadership were those in our study districts seeking to depart from? What new forms of cabinet leadership did we observe supporting the design and implementation of central office transformation, and what premises did those leadership examples reflect? We address those questions in the main sections of this chapter.

PROBLEMS WITH THE CURRENT STATE

Like Superintendent Stow and Principal Supervisor Jones, superintendents and other senior leaders in our study districts did not believe that central office transformation would take root or develop with typical vision-setting or strategic-planning processes that left too many central office staff members unengaged and disconnected. They were concerned that staff experience and expertise were vital resources to the transformation effort but that they typically went untapped and unsupported. And they knew that they too needed support for advancing transformation of their units and aligning efforts across the central office. But historically they had not used their cabinet or other meetings for such strategic collaboration. In this subsection, we elaborate those common concerns. As the chapter title suggests, we distinguish the change strategies typical of many cabinets as reflecting a "telling" approach to leadership because many of them involved issuing directives and otherwise delivering information and did not prompt the kinds of deep change that central office transformation demands.

Staff Throughout the Central Office Typically Had Little Connection to Senior Leaders' Vision or Another Unifying Direction Around Equitable Teaching and Learning

In midsize to large districts, staff members consistently reported that, prior to transformation, superintendents and other cabinet-level leaders frequently launched priorities, strategic plans, or other visions for improving the central office but that they did not feel sufficiently familiar with those initiatives or connected to them. As one central office staff person expressed:

> [In the past] I have had people say, "What is the change that [the superintendent] is talking about? Is there a big change coming?" Like . . . [the superintendent] just talks about it once in a while, and I have no idea what [the superintendent] means. So it has not penetrated the rest of the organization.

Before the launch of the transformation initiative in another district, we observed a superintendent spending most of a day visiting regional meetings of school principals and their supervisors. As she arrived at each meeting, the principal supervisor facilitating the meeting paused the group's activities. The superintendent then spent about ten minutes telling the group that all principals in the district must be "equity warriors" and "excellent instructional leaders," and that she had charged their supervisor with supporting their growth in those areas. She then took a few questions before departing, and principals resumed the meeting activities.

One principal expressed the reactions of many other principals we captured when we asked her what she heard the superintendent say and what it meant to her. She responded, "Can you remind me what she talked about?" Another said, "It's [this district] like the ocean. All this excitement . . . is at the surface. Also, lots of churn. . . . And we [principals] are just down here at the bottom . . . in the dark sometimes."

Some cabinet members also reported that they had often felt disconnected from their superintendent's vision—that they knew what the superintendent was telling them to do but not why, which hampered their understanding for leading the change. As one described, her former superintendent had directed her to lead a major reform of her department, but she did not understand what the reform was or what problems it promised to address. In her words:

> I don't feel like I needed [superintendent] to tell me how to fix it. I needed to understand what [superintendent] was trying to fix and for what purpose. What was [superintendent's] vision . . . the what and the why? What was [superintendent's] intent . . . purpose . . .

overarching, "Here's what I see. Here's what I see central office looking like when we're there," and then I'll figure out how to get us there.

In smaller districts, leaders were concerned that their predecessors generally did not advance a clear vision focused on teaching and learning, let alone equity, leaving staff members with little unifying direction in those areas. For instance, one superintendent assumed the role after the thirty-year tenure of the previous superintendent that largely involved "handshaking, football games, keeping the buses running." She added, "It was like the last fifteen years of school research and reform just skipped over [this district]. . . ." She meant that principals were still operating largely as building managers, and even teachers across the hall from one another spent little time together discussing teaching and learning.

Another superintendent of a smaller district admitted that his own early tenure was marked more by a "culture of community and celebration," adding, "those were much needed things" at the time he arrived in the district. "But our reading and math achievement has been flat and declining for our ELLs [English language learners]." He elaborated:

> We had [a local consulting group] come in and do a kind of audit of our standards and curriculum. . . . And . . . we are all over the map. My staff doesn't see a clear vision or message from me about . . . our core work. I am visible. They trust me. But with the state unveiling its new teacher evaluation system, we are all asking some new questions. What's our vision for instruction? How does it align with the new state expectations? How can we get out ahead of those expectations or start not this far behind?

Staff Expertise and Experience Went Largely Underutilized and Underdeveloped

Our district leaders were also concerned that staff members throughout their central offices had important knowledge and ideas for improving their own work and other parts of the district in service of equitable teaching and learning. However, staff members generally were not encouraged or otherwise supported to solve their day-to-day problems, or elevated to lead for change, and few had received even basic professional development to build their capacity for improved performance. As one central office leader reflected:

> In any industry that survives and thrives, leaders invest in [their] people. They make sure they know the mission. . . . That the mission is *their* mission. And then they invest, invest, invest [in helping their staff members grow to improve their performance]. In education we say, "You are hired. Sit here. There's your boss. Stay in your lane. Do your job."

A leader in another district described, "What we do is we hire people with all this potential and then we stick them in jobs where they don't [have opportunities to] use it." It's a "waste of talent." By this, he meant that staff members know their work better than top management but are rarely tapped for their expertise, which often leads to a misalignment between cabinet-level decisions and the on-the-ground reality of how the system operates. He pointed out the racial dimensions of this dynamic, saying:

> Then you've got, historically, leaders at the top are White . . . a revolving door. But . . . the guts [of the central office] are largely women, Hispanic, Black. . . . We talk about community engagement and . . . voice, but our staff [members] are the community. The district is a top employer in [this region].

He elaborated that when White leadership fails to tap the expertise and leadership of staff members of color, "that's part of the racist culture" where racism "lives and breathes" in our district.

As the comments above suggest, leaders were also concerned that central office transformation required ongoing opportunities for staff members to learn new ways of working but that their central office had not traditionally made those investments. One cabinet member expressed this concern by reflecting on their own early years leading central office transformation:

> My mistake was thinking that with that vague direction about "Go forth and . . . figure out [your job and how to improve it, that staff

would be successful]. . . ." And to have them do it on their own. . . .
[I told them], "You are very smart people or you wouldn't be on
this team, so I don't expect you to come to me with just questions,
questions, questions. I expect you to come to me with solutions. . . ."
But I didn't think anything about the human side of that—what I
was really asking them to do? I didn't think about the skill set either
for them to do it other than that they were smart and they knew
something had to be done.

She elaborated that she had not received training for her cabinet
position, and even though she knew well the struggles of operating
without that support, she was just "passing it [those struggles] down
the line [to staff members]."

Another central office leader similarly reflected:

I was pulled into this job [on the cabinet] straight from a school. . . .
Several of us were with no training. No real job description. . . . You
just get thrown in. It was sink or swim. And I was like, "You have
got to be fucking kidding me." This isn't healthy or sustainable. . . .
And then I found out many of my direct reports had been treading
water like that [with little to no professional development] for years.
I said, "Enough. That's not who we are."

Cabinet Meetings and Cabinet Members' Time Consumed with Nonstrategic Work

Superintendents and other cabinet-level leaders reported that their
cabinet meetings took up too much time and were filled with lengthy
updates on various topics or addressing acute concerns, called "fire
drills" in one district. Such agendas left little time to focus on deeper
strategic work and necessary collaboration in service of central office
transformation. For example, reviews of agendas and meeting minutes
revealed how, in one small district, typical cabinet meetings started
with reports of main discussions and decisions at recent school board
meetings, even though all cabinet members were required to attend
those meetings. Subsequent items involved oral updates on the new
budgeting system, parent complaints, policy around snow-related

school closures, and retirements, all of which were printed in a meeting packet. One cabinet member in a midsize district elaborated:

> You don't even realize that you dread [cabinet meetings]. . . . This one time [in a cabinet meeting] I was emailing my assistant to set up a meeting, and all the people [I needed to meet with] were sitting right there [in the meeting with me]. But that space wasn't ours, and [we knew] not to plan on that time because all the time this one thing comes up and then another and then the agenda gets interrupted for whatever [one school board member] or [another school board member] thinks is the most important thing right then. . . . It's a clown car.

This description of cabinet meetings often mirrored individual cabinet members' days. For example, one member described that, before central office transformation, her calendar was typically double-booked for at least half the week. She would code in blue on her calendar all the meetings and other times focused on her department's core work. Red labels indicated other meetings, which in one particular week included those with union leaders, parents, and vendors that the superintendent had delegated to her, as well as community meetings at which the superintendent wanted to show a "cabinet presence." She said, "Not to be too dramatic . . . but it was red all over . . . a bloodbath."

Another reported that she didn't arrive home before 8 p.m. any day the previous week and that the current week did not look like it would be any better. She added:

> [The superintendent] talks about work-life balance. . . . She said her policy was no email on the weekends . . . which turned out to mean, "Feel free not to respond to other people's emails, but you will hear from me and I expect a quick response." . . . It just got so unmanageable. It was unmanageable to start and then with [the central office transformation initiative], you are building the plane while fixing the one you are flying because it keeps breaking.

A new cabinet member reflected:

> This was my first time on cabinet and I thought it was because I was the new guy [that] my email was lit up with school board members

wanting a meeting or information about this one thing. . . . This one time I told my assistant to batch them [the information requests] and create a block of time on Friday to respond. . . . [You would have thought] I set his hair on fire.

She elaborated that her assistant advised against that strategy, explaining that school board members expected a faster response. Otherwise, they would send multiple follow-ups and eventually involve the superintendent, which just added to everyone's workload and stress.

NEW PREMISES

Leaders across our districts engaged in various shifts to address these and other traditional limitations of cabinet-level leadership. As we elaborate below, those shifts commonly reflected the new premises that cabinets and their members advance central office transformation for equity when they lead the ongoing development and use of a theory of action, foster staff leadership and learning, focus cabinet meeting time on strategy and learning, and bridge and buffer strategically. These changes were like those for principal supervision in their emphasis on cabinets adopting a teaching-and-learning approach to their members' leadership and similarly reflected research on the importance of such an approach to fostering professional growth throughout organizations.

Lead the Ongoing Development and Use of a Theory of Action

Our superintendents did not stop creating visions, strategic priorities, and other expressions of their commitments. But in addition, they and their cabinet members developed theories of action: detailed logic chains identifying how each central office function would operate, singly and in coordination with others, to drive equitable teaching and learning. The theories of action included explicit rationales explaining why those actions were likely to lead to specific outcomes.

These actions reflected research largely from the field of organizational psychology on the value of theories of action to helping organizational actors fundamentally shift their work. For example, such approaches typically prompt participants to articulate what they aim to do and why. As they do so, participants make their thinking explicit to themselves and others in ways that are important to communication and collaboration, and they become better able to see and tap each other's expertise for organizational improvement.[1] This research also suggests the importance of interrogating research and data to inform courses of action and check rationales.[2] Related educational scholarship reveals how theories of action and other parts of inquiry cycles can help various stakeholders work across traditional silos and institutional boundaries and continuously monitor their progress in ways important to their success.[3]

Evidence from our districts suggested that the theories of action about central office transformation were having positive effects. For instance, staff members in one district, across units and levels, consistently used common terms like "flipping the script" from their district's theory of action to describe their work, in this case, how they were shifting from traditional top-down relationships between the central office and schools to a central office–school partnership; to a person, they explained why doing so in their role mattered to equitable teaching and learning. A veteran principal in a small district reported, "This is one of the first times that we [are] all pulling the rope in the same direction." As another put it, "We're all in the same place. . . . It [the theory of action] . . . unites us as one team."

In practice, the theories of action took different forms but included most of the components of theories of action described in the extant research and outlined in table 6.1. First, the theories of action *elaborated how parts of the central office would change in aligned ways to support equitable teaching and learning.* Some also included *evidence of specific underlying problems* that the changes would address and *explicit rationales for why the actions were likely to strengthen equitable teaching and learning.*

For example, one district's theory of action was laid out as a series of workstreams across the central office and indicated "sponsors" (cabinet members accountable for each workstream) and other participants, leading and lagging indicators of success, the specific work shifts likely to lead to those results, rationales for those shifts,

TABLE 6.1 Distinguishing a theory of action

TYPICAL DISTRICT VISIONS	THEORY OF ACTION FOR CENTRAL OFFICE TRANSFORMATION
Broad statements Lists of general activities	A logic map that details how various parts of the central office will change in aligned ways to support equitable teaching and learning. Based on an analysis of specific underlying problems or challenges the theory seeks to address and on explicit evidence-based rationales for why its strategies are likely to address the problems and lead to specific outcomes.
Stakeholders consulted in formulation and sometimes progress monitoring	Developed and continuously refined through ongoing staff and other stakeholder engagement and review of research and data, sometimes from an antiracist approach. Used as a teaching tool to help staff members and others see their specific contribution to a system of support for equitable teaching and learning.

and participants' progress toward them. As in Superintendent Stow's district, a unifying graphic illustrated specific ways that the individual workstreams depended on each other for their success.

In another district, the unit-specific theories of action were organized around the four "pillars" and outcomes of the district's five-year strategic plan, with elaborated rationales for why those theories were consistent with the pillars and would likely address particular inequities. As a cabinet member explained:

> Without the theory of action [for my unit] the strat plan is just a document . . . like a brochure for the district that you hand out at community meetings. . . . And without the strat plan, the theory of action can get too out there. . . . We took the strategic plan, and my staff [members] and I did a deep dive into how we are falling short [of its equity goals]. . . . Then we jumped off from there to identify specific changes related to the pillars we could do to move the needle. . . . With just the pillars, we are operating at 30,000 feet . . . with just a theory of action we could just be going through the motions. . . . The self-assessment really solidified our why. . . .

Helped us connect problems we care about and see the theory of action as the path forward.

One superintendent opened a meeting with her cabinet on the development of their theory of action by reviewing a protocol that guided members in first identifying the underlying problems they wanted their theory of action to address. In her words to her staff, the protocol:

> is going to help us work together to make sure we are getting the problem right, so as we move through the process, we can keep coming back to, "Are we [focused] on the right things?" So [we start with], "What's the problem of student learning [that is prompting us to engage in central office reform]?" And then you say, "Okay, what do teachers have to do differently to address that?" And then we say, "What do principals and we as [cabinet] leaders need to do differently to get teachers to do that thing to address it? . . . What do both of us [principals and central office staff members] have to do differently or know that we don't know now to enable teachers to change their practice?"

District leaders also *engaged staff and other stakeholders with research and data to develop and continuously refine their theories of action*, sometimes from an antiracist approach. A cabinet member explained the importance of such engagement, saying that staff members and other stakeholders sometimes have "misconceptions" about how the "central office does, could, and should operate." They then bring those to our meetings about the theory of action work, and "it becomes a kind of blame game rather than problem solving" activity. She added that many antiracist approaches advocated for community engagement as a centerpiece. She continued:

> I agree with that . . . but if you just listen [to stakeholders] and don't . . . look at the data, look at the research on the solutions someone says will save us all, you stay in a place of blame and argument [over whose input matters more]. That pretty much sums up . . . our early meetings [about developing our theory of action]. Now, we bring evidence into the conversation to say, "We hear you.

We need to hear you. And here's some data we can look at together. What do we make of it? Why do we think this one thing is a solution? Let's look at the research together and decide together with some shared evidence. . . ." That starts to shift the conversation from blame to problem-solving.

One superintendent opened a retreat with her leadership team by prompting members to work in small groups to interpret sets of student learning data using guiding prompts such as, "What main trends do the data reveal? Whose voices are mainly represented in the data, and what does that mean about what the data let us see? What do we not learn—for example, about the strengths of our students of color—and how can we learn more?" She then facilitated the whole group in coming to agreement about a few initial claims about the current state of student learning and questions to investigate further to ensure that the claims centered the strengths of historically marginalized students. The team reconvened to examine the new data and refine their claims. In subsequent meetings, the team identified claims they wanted to be making about their students' learning in three years and used a protocol to develop a theory of action for their own work with shifts they could show were likely to help the district realize those new targets.

Leaders in three districts also used data from extensive annual satisfaction surveys to inform adjustments in their theories of action. In one instance, although their theory of action rested on what cabinet leaders considered a clear logic connecting teacher learning communities with advancing equitable teaching and learning, survey results showed that, on average, teachers and principals did not perceive the emerging communities as aligned with those results. A project team then investigated that finding further and identified recommended shifts not in the theory of action itself but in its execution.

In some districts, leaders drew on research to inform which courses of action to include in the theories of action. For instance, leaders in one midsize district hosted a series of learning sessions for cabinet members to review our initial research findings about central office transformation and subsequently used them to ground the development of theories of action in T&L and HR. One chief of schools had his principal supervisors review our research on that role and reflect on how their existing theory of action emphasized their use of teaching-and-learning moves in their one-on-one coaching but not also helping principals lead their own learning or principal development in learning communities.[4] They subsequently revised their theory of action to amplify those research-based aspects and dedicated team meeting time to receiving feedback on their use of them in their practice.

One superintendent of a small district facilitated a summer retreat with principals and T&L staff members to develop a theory of action focusing the principalship and principal supervision on equity-focused instructional leadership. The superintendent began by prompting participants to discuss, in small and large groups, how they understood the relationship between the principalship and improved instruction, especially for their district's historically marginalized students. A second set of prompts guided participants in reviewing research on the principalship as instructional leadership, culturally responsive leadership, and principal supervision. The group then organized their ideas into a theory of action defining the principal supervisor–principal relationship in ways consistent with the research and how that relationship mattered to high-quality teaching and ultimately student learning.

As the examples above suggest, cabinet leaders also *used their theories of action as a teaching tool*; while they engaged staff members and other stakeholders in developing and revisiting the theories of action, cabinet leaders were also helping them learn about their district's strategic direction and their essential roles in it. One cabinet member explained that in the past, when a superintendent launched a new vision:

> [Their approach was] scaring the shit out of people [through downsizing departments and letting staff go]. And then people say, "Oh, I guess it's a new day. . . ." The other way . . . is to assume the best about the human beings that are in your organization. And . . . try to help them get engaged in "Why do we need to change?" And build a case for change and bring the people along with you.

This leader went on to describe how they used the district's overall theory of action as a teaching tool in those ways:

> [We] sit down [with each staff person] and figure out how their job related to student achievement. Each one of us had to do that. And it was very difficult for some people on my staff. I remember my secretary said, "Well, I don't have anything to do with it." I said, "Well if you don't, then go home. . . . Go home and think about it and come back." And so she did and she says, "Well, you know, I did do the [coordination of resources for the school board], and if I don't do it well, then the board gets mad and maybe they won't approve something. . . ." Bingo—there you go. . . . That's our first business: How do we make ourselves relevant to schools?

A superintendent of a small district similarly described using their theory of action with staff members:

> We had a series of meetings . . . where I gave all of the district office folks opportunities to think about their job, and what they do here, and its impacts on various things in the theory of action. And we did this over about a six- to eight-month period. About ways that the things they do help the district's teaching and learning or hinder it. And for many of them, it was the first time of ever even thinking about stuff like that.

The success of many aspects of central office transformation depended on shifts in the principalship, and several cabinet members consistently used their theories of action to build principals' understanding of their role in central office transformation. As one explained:

> I've been going out . . . to talk to principals and staff. . . . I want to hear what people are saying. And what I've realized is most people, including principals, like when I really explain what was the theory of action behind [the reform] and how it is an equity strategy and how decisions they don't even realize they have been making can interfere with that outcome.

In one meeting, she engaged principals in an activity to help them see that, despite progress in the central office with transforming HR, principals were allocating staff members in ways that ran counter to the reforms and therefore the district's equity goals. Principals then began drafting new parts of HR's theory of action to specify how and why shifts in the principalship and HR were mutually reinforcing.

Some superintendents also recognized the importance of continuously engaging their own cabinet in understanding the theory of action. As one superintendent explained:

> Trying to get everybody on the same page about what the theory of action is, especially if the theory of action is complex, which ours is, is challenging. Even at this level, we go over them over time, and each time we all get a little clearer about what the other is doing and what's possible for them [other units], which starts to expand our thinking [about what's possible in our unit].

An executive coach working in a small distinct shared that the superintendent had worked with her cabinet to develop the initial theory of action, but they had to rewrite it within the first year:

> Halfway through the first year, we were at a [cabinet] meeting and . . . the superintendent . . . said, "You know what? I think we need to relook at this problem of practice and theory of action because I think we just did an assignment. I think we need to do this better and make it our own." And they went back, and the focus didn't change that much, but their approach to it did, and then their strategies began to be more meaningful and a little deeper thought put into them. . . . That's when they started being a better team . . . to understand that this has to be their real work.

Foster Staff Leadership and Learning

Cabinet members also helped staff members lead the implementation of central office transformation, and they supported staff members learning how to do so. Their actions reflected research cited in chapter 5 on the importance of tapping and cultivating leadership and knowledge at every level of an organization in service of organizational performance, the transformative agency of staff members as a key resource for reinventing long-standing work, and the engagement of historically marginalized community members in educational improvement.[5]

We analyzed the growth of central office staff members along specific practices involved in central office transformation, and our data also supported this premise. We found varying levels of change in staff practice, including no engagement, regression, persistence, and growth. Staff members exhibited the most growth when they led their own learning or worked closely with their superintendents as main leaders of their learning—not when receiving outside coaching, regardless of coaching quality.[6]

In the last subsection of chapter 5, we described various instances of cabinet members fostering the leadership of operational staff members to improve their work processes. As another example, most principals and central office staff members in one district pointed to the same HR analyst as, in the words of one principal, "the one you want" supporting you with personnel matters, and, as noted in chapter 3, some principals developed workarounds to secure her assistance. That analyst told us that, for years, she had few opportunities even to discuss with others how she worked with principals. As part of the central office transformation process, the new head of HR helped her lead sessions with colleagues about how to help principals use staffing to drive equitable teaching and learning. For instance, in one meeting she guided other HR analysts through examples from her own practice that she thought reflected varying degrees of success. Participants used the cases as jumping off points to develop an initial set of criteria to ground the redesign of the teacher hiring process.

As these examples suggest, leaders provided opportunities for staff members to learn how to lead parts of central office transformation, even while the leaders themselves were learning how to do so. As one cabinet member expressed, "I think one of the things that's [been] successful is that the whole is greater than the sum of its parts. That we really capitalize on [our] . . . shared learning [so the work can] . . . evolve and be what it needs to be at the time." In the words of another:

> You have to rely on your team to get the work done, just like a princi-
> pal in a school [does with their teachers and support staff]. You must
> make time for them. . . . You must plan with them and make sure
> that everyone understands—and I mean planning down . . . to the
> who, the what, the when, and the how. You cannot escape that. You
> cannot take it for granted that just because people are willing, they're
> smart, loyal to the district, and . . . they've been here [that] they know
> [what to do]. That you can leave that alone. They need feedback. . . .
> They need that sacred time with you. . . . They also need validation.

Several superintendents of small districts stood out in our data for their intensive support of staff members learning to lead central office transformation. For example, one superintendent led a series of meetings with her staff members in response to their feedback that they were struggling to integrate their districtwide definition of equitable teaching and learning into the work of their units. In framing the first meeting, she explained, "We have all been struggling a bit with this [anchoring our work to the teaching-and-learning framework]. As a district, where can we get our arms around something this year and see if we can try out this for our leadership team?" She then modeled her thinking behind how focusing on one aspect of the framework could provide a way forward. At one point, she explained:

> One of the elements of [the instructional framework] is around
> engagement and student talk. What if we say "Okay, let's just at
> least talk about that?" And then, as leaders, how can we collect
> data on . . . what that means for students and teachers and then
> principals and then our [central office] work?

A protocol then guided staff members to consider the extent to which the work of their units currently supported that focus, to collect data on the pros and cons of their current state, and to review selected research on ways to move forward. At the next two meetings, staff members shared the results for feedback and collaborated on next steps.

A cabinet member in a midsize district described how she coached staff:

> I spent time with each person . . . on different systems stuff . . . [related to leading central office transformation to] break down the various areas of things that people should know. . . . And part of it is to teach them not only about those things but to take them on at least one school visit so you see . . . what does that actually mean to be at a school and how do you approach that relationship . . . especially when things come up in the gray areas.

By that, she meant that one of her main teaching points with staff members was how central office transformation was not just about improving their long-standing work but identifying new ways to support equitable teaching and learning in schools. She said that those experiences helped them understand the need for growing their skills in leading project teams, and she then trained them in certain project management methods.

Focus Cabinet Meeting Time on Strategy and Learning

Many of our superintendents shifted their cabinet meetings from information-sharing or crisis-management sessions to settings where they collaborated on central office transformation strategy and learned together how to lead it forward. One superintendent explained that they aimed to transform their cabinet alongside the rest of the central office in these ways:

> Because we wanted to shift the focus from the management things to what we were all about, which was teaching and learning. Because we weren't getting the results and we knew we wouldn't get the results . . . unless we worked together as a [cabinet] team to get there.

Another said:

> You can't ask staff to align their work with . . . [equitable teaching and learning] if we don't change . . . cabinet. All of what we do trickles down, like it or not. . . . [When our] meetings keep focusing

on the same go around and make announcements, . . . that becomes
the other meetings [that cabinet members run in their units]. So
[now] we walk the talk and then people [cabinet members] experience something really different [in the cabinet meetings] and then
they start to ask questions like, "Why are we meeting? Can this just
be an email . . . ?" We are seeing that now. . . . [A cabinet member]
just showed me their staff meeting plan [for their unit] that isn't
once a week all morning . . . it starts with the workflow and then
meetings are built in to support that, what we call "just-in-time"
meetings instead of "all-the-time" meetings . . . [or] meetings for
the sake of meetings.

Their efforts in this regard were consistent with various research
in education and other fields about the importance of ongoing collaborative learning opportunities to leadership of complex change
processes.[7] Some shifts in cabinet interactions also reflected features
of communities of practice—such as tapping all members as learning resources and learning through participation—as elaborated in
previous chapters.[8]

As an example, for his cabinet meetings, one superintendent
developed what he called a "scope and sequence"—a term refer-
ring to an intentional progression of a curriculum. The scope and
sequence included learning goals for the cabinet team over the course
of the year and activities to help them progress. For instance, the
learning goals for his October cabinet meetings one year focused on
deepening members' understanding of instructional frameworks and
how to use them to guide work across the central office. Activities
included discussions with leaders from another district that had made
progress in that area, a self-assessment of unit readiness, and work
with an outside facilitator to identify next steps.

Another superintendent's cabinet meetings engaged members
in rotating through different central office units, with a protocol for
members to share their progress on central office transformation, sticking points, and questions for feedback. They engaged in a quarterly
activity, similar to the one featured in the chapter-opening vignette, to
check for alignment and interdependencies across units. This district's

superintendent explained that, to create that learning time for her executive team, she charged her assistant with preparing a weekly memo with the standing information items and updates that had consumed cabinet meetings in the past; she said, "You keep on top of those . . . if it's something you can just put in writing, you write it and expect your people to read it . . . and that's how we protect our [cabinet] time."

In a smaller district, where the superintendent also served as the principal supervisor and all school principals sat on cabinet, the superintendent reorganized his cabinet time to include a short weekly "items meeting," where they discussed various issues, and two principal learning community meetings. The latter convened at a rotating school site and focused on principals' growth as instructional leaders, as we described in chapter 4.

For example, at one meeting, the cabinet team spent the morning at a school site observing the principal and several lead teachers as they coached teachers in real time in their classrooms around a new mathematics curriculum. That meeting opened with an outside facilitator helping the group consider the importance of principals at all school levels understanding the curriculum and key roles for principals in supporting teacher learning around it. The group then conducted classroom observations focused on both the quality of teaching and the principals' leadership of teacher learning, provided feedback to the host principal, and discussed implications for their own work. For instance, the operations director noted the considerable amount of time that the host principal needed for that work with teachers and planned to share what she observed with her staff to deepen their understanding of the importance of their helping principals protect that time.

Bridge Strategically to External and Internal Resources and Buffer Against Distractions

Cabinet members also intentionally bridged or connected to various resources that promised to fuel central office transformation for equity while also buffering themselves from demands that did not. Their efforts were like those of the principal supervisors we highlighted in chapter 4, and they were likewise consistent with research from sociocultural learning theory on the importance of managing the boundaries of learning communities.[9] Sociological research on organizations also emphasizes the strategic function of boundary spanning—including connecting organizations to resources, maintaining boundaries, and helping with communication across boundaries—as essential to organizational innovation and performance.[10]

In practice, many of the *bridging* efforts involved the superintendent and cabinet members proactively engaging funders and policy makers—tapping them for advice and encouraging them to invest in their strategic priorities around central office transformation. As one cabinet member described, the superintendent convened and led an informal advisory team "of the top CEOs in the city. . . . She would meet with them once a quarter. And they would *really* talk about things. . . . They would give her that kind of wisdom that they get from those places [the organizations and sectors they lead]."

In another district, the chief operating officer facilitated regular meetings of leaders from the private philanthropic community to seek their advice and their political and financial support for their central office transformation process. We observed several of these meetings, at which central office staff members provided updates on their progress; engaged funders in discussions about next steps; and challenged funders to consider how they might work together to support the district's ongoing efforts, especially in light of persistently large budget shortfalls in that district and state.[11]

As one central office participant described, "It creates a kind of friendly competition" where the funders want to hear the successes of their own investments, and "they are . . . comparing themselves" to each other and "who made the smartest investment, . . . which has fueled interest and investment." Another explained, "The time savings is phenomenal." She elaborated that, with the funders all in the same room, they can make one "pitch" and "guide the funders' giving" instead of waiting to see their priorities for that year. "We show them what we need . . . and what's important. They come and see others interested and they want in."

As noted in chapter 5, cabinet leaders proactively engaged unions as partners and key knowledge resources. In two districts, those partnerships also involved the teachers' union. As one union leader explained, "Some people are surprised" by the teachers' union's ardent support for central office transformation, but for us, "it was a no brainer. Everything [involved in central office transformation] is about elevating teachers and their professionalism and support. . . . Making sure teachers have what they need to succeed." One T&L director shared that, at first, union leadership was suspicious. But "we kept going back and back," inviting them to be on the work teams. "Eventually they started to trust that it's a new day." He added:

> We didn't touch the [teachers' union] contract. We never made it about that. . . . We looked at all we could already do within current [contract] terms . . . and . . . instead of our usual pushing things out to them [e.g., new reform strategies or requirements], we invited them in [to help reform the central office].

Cabinet leaders also *buffered* or shielded their meetings and other work time from historically frequent interruptions by school board representatives, vendors, and community members. The most common buffering strategy across the larger districts was the creation of a chief of staff position to focus on managing external relations, especially with the school board. As one described:

> [I am] the administrative liaison with the board. I help manage their expectations, help keep them in their role as policy makers. . . . I do . . . all the backdrop for the board meetings. All of the action items . . . everything . . . before it gets to the board, it comes through me. . . . I ensure that everything that comes up to the board, first of all, should come to the board and that they're not addressing issues that they should not be. We had a long history of things going to the board that really should not have gone there but went there because of practice. And also then making sure that they make sense.

He elaborated that, early in his tenure, board members reached out to "any and all" district staff members and consumed hours every week.

His initial strategy for "disciplining the board" was to respond rapidly so board members would see him as their preferred contact. He continued:

> A protocol was agreed upon with the board [and the superinten-dent] . . . that their questions and concerns would come to me. And it took a while for them to get with it [the protocol]. . . . I started to rein them in . . . helped them understand that do they really need this one answer before the board meeting [or can it wait until the meeting] . . . and do you really need it at all?

In smaller systems, the superintendents generally described playing that buffering role. On superintendent said:

> I specifically keep the board from taking staff time off of the work that they are supposed to be doing. . . . I help the board members obtain their constituency-driven goals or whatever their goals are with the minimum disruption to the schools and central office. . . . For example, sometimes . . . a parent will call them or send them a letter, and in the past, they would go directly to the principal or the principal's supervisor. [And they would say,] "Well, explain this to me or what's going on." Well now, they can't do that. They have to come to me.

These leaders played similar roles with vendors. In the words of one:

> There will be vendors that want to bring in a product to show the principals. No, that's not the way we do it. We have a mechanism for doing that. Or they'll want to pop into schools. No. It's a public place, but it's not a place for you to just go and be disruptive.

This superintendent went on to explain that he had his secretary log all the vendor calls for his review once a week, saying, "It takes disci-pline from all of us. . . . Every call I take interrupts my instructional focus too . . . and . . . I try to model that [for my staff]."

Over time, cabinet's ongoing leadership of central office trans-formation led to deeper implementation, which itself became a key strategy for bridging and buffering in service of its own goals. As one cabinet member put it, "The more we demonstrated results, the more they [funders and policy makers] got on board to support our direction" and the less they "presented distractions." In addition, as T&L built their own mechanisms for brokering vendors, as we discussed in chapter 2, outside organizations increasingly channeled their inquiries through that process. As HR improved its strategic support for principals and teachers in ways we describe in chapter 3, some district leaders pointed to a decrease in the number of complaints and conduct matters that district leaders and staff members had to manage, further freeing their time for equitable teaching and learning. Per chapter 4, principal supervisors' efforts to buffer their own time and that of their principals' meetings reinforced for school board directors, community members, and others the importance of their instructional leadership focus. And as operations units increasingly drew on their staff members' expertise, as we discussed in chapter 5, they strengthened community engagement and other resources for central office transformation for equity.

SUMMARY

When the superintendent and cabinet-level leaders talked about every single central office staff person mattering to the success of central office transformation for equity, they were also talking about their own roles as well as their use of cabinet time. School and central office staff members traditionally felt disconnected from their superintendent's cabinet and their priorities. Cabinet meetings were consumed with various matters, many of which cabinet leaders believed did not require a meeting and provided little time and support for the kind of coordination and mutual learning that central office transformation required. They also faced various intrusions on their own time. As part of central office transformation, they used a theory-of-action approach to engage stakeholders throughout the district in developing and implementing the district's vision for advancing equitable teaching and learning. They also sought to walk their own talk by focusing their cabinet and individual time on supporting the leadership and learning of staff members—including themselves—toward that vision. Their bridging and buffering efforts helped them do so while also marshalling important resources for advancing their work.

Superintendent interns like Jones in the chapter-opening vignette made careful study of this kind of cabinet-level leadership as well as other aspects of central office transformation. They planned to use the lessons they learned to advance their own central office transformation initiative. What are the key lessons the experiences of our study districts offer to the field? What are promising future directions that educational leaders and researchers might consider to innovate forward? We address those questions in the concluding chapter.

CHAPTER 7

From What We Know to What's Next

In the preceding chapters, we shared our main findings from several research studies and many district partnerships that address an essential question at the heart of efforts to realize educational equity: What do school district central offices do when they support equitable teaching and learning? To address that question, we stood on the shoulders of other equity researchers whose work helped us to appreciate how the individual, interpersonal, and organizational levels of central offices have historically perpetuated racism and other inequities and to train our attention on the institutional level that undergirds and fuels the others. With that focus, we sought district leaders who understood the fundamental mismatch between their long-standing central offices and what equitable teaching and learning takes, specifically at the institutional level of values, norms, and taken-for-granted assumptions, which we call "premises." We walked alongside them as they tackled that institutional problem. We directly observed them in real time as they set aside parts of their current central office and built new ones grounded in premises that reflected that the core purpose of central offices should be to foster equitable teaching and learning. For example, one key premise evident in the shifts in Teaching and Learning (T&L) units was that T&L units advance equitable teaching and learning when they *align and coordinate all their work around a common set of standards defining equitable teaching and learning with culturally responsive practices as integral parts.* And we were able to connect their new work, consistent with this and the other premises, with actual improvements in support of equitable teaching and learning.

The experience of our study and partner districts suggests that they and others would do well to focus their equity efforts on institutional-level changes in their central offices. Shifting premises provides one way to think about what that focus means: fundamental pivots in the underlying assumptions that drive daily work across the central office. And the specific premises we share in this book offer concrete ways forward: a new foundational set of assumptions about the essential purpose of a central office as a driver of educational equity. Like a new foundation, these premises can help leaders and staff members shape central office work into new forms. Now, central office leaders do not need to face the challenge of a completely blank page when seeking to transform their central offices; they can use the premises we share in this book as anchors for their own efforts.

These premises directly address many though not all parts of a central office, however. For example, the premises about T&L and Human Resources (HR) that we had data to support sufficiently mainly address teacher professional development and staffing. But leaders can use the premises to identify new ways of working in areas we did not discuss. For instance, leaders in one district took the finding about the importance of teacher learning in teams and recast it to call for *educator* learning teams that included certified teachers and also paraprofessionals and specialists. Another district reviewed the findings about teacher recruitment and selection and used them to inform the transformation of the recruitment and selection of principals.

Even with the new premises and examples of how other districts realized them in practice, central office transformation for equitable teaching and learning is hardly easy work. Our leaders are not short on metaphors to capture these challenges. Many are variations on the old idiom "building the plane while flying it" and refer to the dynamic of having to run their current systems while creating the systems they need to advance equitable teaching and learning. Other metaphors conjure up different images, as when one leader said that her leadership of central office transformation sometimes makes her feel "I'm like the dog riding the bike with the cat juggling the mice." But in her words, "Once you see it, you can't unsee it [the mismatch between the current and necessary ways of working], and you realize you have been leading your systems in the wrong direction, and you will continue to be a major part of the problem if you don't act, as painful as that can be sometimes to admit."

Her experiences and those of other leaders with whom we have worked over the years offer many lessons for districts seeking to make these important but also challenging shifts. In the next section, we share some of those lessons organized in the form of questions that district leaders frequently ask us about how to move forward. Then we identify future directions for other stakeholders, including intermediary and school support organizations, funders, policy makers, and researchers, to help district leaders get started, stay the course, and achieve success.

SOME FAQs ABOUT CENTRAL OFFICE TRANSFORMATION FOR EQUITY

Where Do We Start?

When we were just beginning this program of research about fifteen years ago, our answer was consistent with what we saw district leaders doing: start with a blank page. As discussed in the introduction to this book, however, that starting place is not always the right one to spark leaders' imagination about what a fundamentally different, truly equity-centered central office could look like, especially because many central office leaders secured their positions precisely for their proficiency with the current system as-is.

Now we say, *use the research*. And we have observed several ways that district leaders have done so with success. For one, district leaders have used the research to *expand their imaginations* and those of their staff members regarding what is possible with their central office. We often start cabinet learning sessions, for example, with the chapter-opening vignettes for that purpose. Sometimes participants find ideas in the vignettes that had long resonated with them but that they had abandoned somewhere along the way, and those portraits help them return to those ideas with new motivation. Other staff members tell us that, before they encountered the research, they only knew the systems where they had worked and that the research helped them, in the words of one, "want things that never would have occurred to me to want." Taking time to expand people's imaginations in these and other ways can be an important first step in engaging them as leaders of central office transformation, as we discussed in chapter 6.

Two, leaders we work with *design from the specific, new premises we shared in these chapters*, and we recommend others do the same. In response to that suggestion, some leaders look at us side-eyed, with an expression that says, "That is too many things to be a starting place." We agree that the notion of a "starting place" suggests something narrower and more modest, such as a problem of practice that's become the cornerstone of many common change processes in education. But as we discussed in chapter 1, when it comes to fundamental systemic change, the primary units of change are the premises that underlie current work. We find that when leaders engage staff members in understanding the premises and seeing the depths of the mismatches between those premises and their current work, staff members develop important motivation and anchors for moving forward, and otherwise see change as possible and doable.

In addition, as we have tried to indicate within and in the transitions between chapters, most of the shifts we chronicle here are interdependent. For example, in our study districts, HR built its capacity to staff teacher teams thanks in part to T&L pivoting to make teacher teams the main unit of teacher development. And T&L's ability to do the latter depended in part on HR strategically staffing teacher teams to take the onus off district-provided teacher professional development as the main lever of teacher growth. Therefore, we recommend district leaders understand the findings we share here as an ecosystem: any new premise they introduce in one part of their central office will invariably affect the other parts—and depend on aligned shifts in the others—especially over time. The key is to begin someplace and follow which changes seem most important to advancing the first work and then to evolve from there.

For instance, many districts start with transformation of principal supervision, but if they do not then move to create aligned shifts in other central office units, principal supervisors tend to regress to traditional conceptions of their roles. Some leaders have overcome that predictable outcome by observing the detractors to principal supervisors' instructional focus and moving swiftly to initiate transformation there as their next priority.

Three, our findings do not address the entire central office, however, and our districts' successes suggest districts *avoid starting with the aspects of central offices not covered in this book.* For instance, most of our districts did not pursue budget reforms; in those that did, we did not find a clear connection between their budgeting strategies and advancing central office transformation or otherwise supporting equitable teaching and learning. Clarifying the essential central office work that a budget should support appeared to be an important step *before* pursuing transformation of the budget system. Also, for example, our districts did not engage in transformation of special education services. Chances are, the premise changes we did observe in T&L could have provided an important foundation for fundamental shifts in special education services, but given tight regulations and sometimes contentious politics in that area, leaders likely did well by not starting there.

Four, leaders can start with the research by helping cabinet members *build theories of action for how each central office unit, individually and together, supports equitable teaching and learning with the research-based premises as initial anchors.* In chapter 6, we discussed in detail the importance of a theory of action to supporting central office transformation for equity—for example, by enabling each staff person to see themselves as an essential part of the change by participating in theory of action development and ongoing refinement and implementation.

Pursuing small wins in the context of a broader research-based theory of action has helped some districts marshal various stakeholder support for and engagement in the deeper long-term work of central office transformation. For example, the home-run projects we discussed in chapter 6 were designed in part to demonstrate for principals that central office transformation meant new support for their growth as instructional leaders and to encourage them to support the work ahead. Leaders in that district took care to frame those and other discrete projects as just that: initial fixes and not the broader central office transformation effort. In districts where leaders did not provide that framing, staff sometimes confused the small wins with central office transformation itself, which stalled progress.

Whether or not you use the research, if your district does not have cabinet leaders with the intrinsic motivation to move central office transformation forward, do not start with them; instead, *go with the ready leaders* and *consider restaffing your cabinet with those leaders.* For example, one superintendent charged her cabinet with leading central office transformation and had us work with them to understand the research and build theories of action and processes for redesigning their core work. But two key cabinet members did not engage with the research and were adamant that they did not agree with it. When we raised concerns about buy-in with the superintendent, she told us that was not an issue because she mandated that they lead it. However, central office transformation is such complex, labor-intensive change that mandates only go so far, and the cabinet members successfully delayed their engagement, which ultimately stymied the whole initiative when their units presented persistent roadblocks to changes in other units.

How Much Will It Cost?

The shifts we describe in this book were mostly, and in some places entirely, cost-neutral because they involved the elimination of old work and the redirection of existing resources to the new work. In the words of one HR leader, "If [central office transformation] isn't cost neutral, then you are doing it wrong." He meant that, if leaders truly understand that central office transformation is about shutting down long-standing ways of working and replacing them with new ones, then the funding necessary for the latter is already in central office budgets but currently misallocated. Another district leader explained, "We have the money we need in our budget . . . it's just that we haven't found a reason to use it differently." As we noted, especially in chapter 5, districts that have proceeded in this mode have actually realized cost savings.

When Is the Right Time to Start? And Where Are We Supposed to Find the Time?

Many central office leaders committed to central office transformation for equitable teaching and learning never take the first step in part because they can always find reasons to delay. In our work with central office leaders over the years, we consistently find the beginning of the school year is consumed with start-of-year demands; by the time those die down, it's holiday season and fatigue is high. January and February sometimes bring with them some New Year optimism and a lightening of schedules. But March is budget season, which in some ways is precisely the occasion to rethink next years' priorities. But if that thinking doesn't start until March, time quickly runs out before budgets and staffing plans are due. After that, staff members are closing down the school year—completing evaluations, reconciling budgets, and otherwise preoccupied with their current work. Summer could be a good time for deeper planning, but many central office leaders and staff members take much needed vacations in July, and by August, people are anticipating the start of the year ahead. Rinse and repeat.

And throughout the year, time is at a premium. As we have discussed throughout this book, the current state in many districts is characterized by workloads that far exceed available time. In some districts, cabinet members work most evenings and weekends so they will have a chance of staying on top of running their current systems. How are they supposed to add central office transformation on top of everything else?

The leaders that have advanced central office transformation have not waited for a time better than the present; they have made that approach a reality in part by shutting old work down, even before they were certain what to do instead. For instance, one chief academic officer came to realize that her district's long-standing school improvement planning process was so misaligned with equitable teaching and learning that she charged a design team with transforming it. In the meantime, she suspended the then-current process, saying, "I realize it's not even worth doing, so why keep doing it." As we discussed in chapter 6, the superintendent of a small district simply discontinued the routine of lengthy reports in cabinet meetings and replaced them with learning activities. He reflected:

> Sometimes it's amazing how everyone holds on to things [long-standing work] and says, "We can't change" or "It's against . . . rules." But then you do put a stop to things and, nothing [bad happens]. . . . Nothing but recovered time and maybe fewer headaches.

How Can Others Help?

Intermediary, technical assistance, and other school support organizations. These external organizations could add value to district central office transformation efforts, but doing so likely will require fundamental shifts in *their* long-standing ways of working. First, leaders of those organizations can build their knowledge and other capacity to support leadership of central office transformation specifically. Although central office leadership differs from school leadership in countless ways, we have seen too many staff members of these external organizations take their strategies and tools from their work with schools and simply use them when working with the central office. Or they provide generic forms of executive coaching that are not well-aligned with the dynamics of leading fundamental systemic change for equity in a school district central office environment. As a result, we have observed that the work of these organizations in central offices is too often costly with few returns. How can intermediary, technical assistance, and other support organizations avoid those missteps and create more relevant assistance for central office leaders of central office transformation?

In the process, how can they ensure that they do not step in and facilitate central office transformation *for* central office leaders and instead build internal leadership capacity to move the work forward? The findings we shared in chapter 6 reinforce the importance of internal leadership for central office transformation and the limited impact of external coaching that does not build internal leadership capacity. But building internal leadership capacity runs counter to standard business strategies in some external organizations such as ensuring their high rather than low visibility and securing large district contracts rather than essentially working themselves out of a job from day one. To do better with central office transformation for equity, many of these external organizations may need to shift their basic budget models.

These external organizations will also need to build their capacity for nimble, cross-silo work in central offices. As we have noted throughout this book, central office transformation progresses when central office leaders move on multiple fronts at once and work across traditional units and intra-unit boundaries. Outside organizations can actually interfere with central office progress when their coaching and tools focus on improvement within rather than across those divides. Our own ability to support district leaders with central office transformation has benefitted from our ability to pivot.

For example, in one district, we spent several months working closely with the chief academic officer and T&L while lightly supporting the head of HR, frequently sharing knowledge of the priorities and progress of all involved and facilitating their communication and collaboration. As leadership capacity in T&L grew, we shifted to deeper work within HR. Because we were funded by outside grants we secured ourselves, we did not have to wait to renegotiate a district contract or worry about deviating from pre-planned billable hours.

Policy makers and philanthropic leaders. As we noted in chapter 1, building school district central office capacity to lead for equitable teaching and learning has not been a long-standing investment area for federal and state agencies or for private philanthropic foundations. But research and experience continue to point to central office leadership as essential for those results, and policy makers and philanthropic leaders can help support it. First, they can serve as important thought partners for superintendents and cabinet members, as they did in our study districts, especially around the development and initial implementation of theories of action. They did so not by monitoring or directing but learning alongside district leaders and helping them celebrate successes and stay the course during setbacks.

Second, while central office transformation should be cost neutral, strategic public and philanthropic investments can help propel the work forward. For example, some districts have used such funding to conduct site visits in districts further along in central office transformation and to attend various conferences where they received vital feedback on their work from colleagues across the country. At least two national foundations we know have invested in networks of district leaders to learn about central office transformation research and receive peer accountability and support for moving it forward.

Federal and state policy makers and philanthropic leaders might consider that the siloed and nonstrategic operation of central offices is partly a legacy of federal and state policy making and private funding for discrete programs and initiatives, and seek to interrupt that legacy. For example, policy guidance and funding could support the development of school improvement planning processes that help central offices strategically support schools across content areas and programs in the ways we described in chapter 2. The Wallace Foundation's equity-focused principal pipeline initiative provides a promising example of a philanthropic foundation making a relatively long-term strategic investment in creating aligned systems of support across a principal's career in ways consistent with central office transformation.

Private and public funders alike can also support the ongoing generation and use of knowledge to guide central office transformation for equitable teaching and learning. For example, we recommend funders invest in research programs that promise to illuminate positive cases of leaders engaging in the challenging work of uprooting and reinventing their central offices as engines of educational equity. If our research is any guide, such studies will generate vast amounts of data that require time to mine and translate into findings and knowledge resources for the field. Our research would not have been possible without support from understanding funders who provided us with longer time horizons for producing reports of findings than they may have traditionally expected. Public and private funders could encourage researchers to ensure that they build into their research budgets the support needed for dedicated data analysis and writing time.

Researchers. As we have emphasized, research can be a vital resource for central office transformation for equitable teaching and learning by providing an essential foundation as well as jumping off points for that challenging work. Our experience suggests that generating such knowledge requires researchers to embed themselves inside central offices to observe central office transformation as it unfolds. For instance, our methods have included attending meetings as well as walking busy central office leaders to their cars to squeeze in a few minutes of conversation, talking with them by phone on their commutes home, reading their emails (with permission, of course), shadowing them throughout their day, and otherwise putting ourselves in places where we could see their work unfold in real time. Forging formal research practice partnerships with districts has also helped us establish the necessary collaborations and access, and other researchers may find similar success with that approach.

Scholars of educational equity have tended to focus on schools or shifts in individual behaviors and policies, and many have not seen core central office work as an important main area of study. As one prestigious equity scholar once asked us, skeptically, when we were first launching this research program, "If you care about equity, why would you study central offices?" We hope our work offers some inspiration to the next generation of equity scholars to consider the institutional roots of racism and other inequities *within central offices*—and to take a strengths-based approach to their work. After all, we already know that central offices are riddled with inequities. What we *need* to know is what it looks like when central offices advance equitable teaching and learning. A research agenda on the latter requires identifying district leaders pursuing fundamental systemic central office shifts to support those results; it also requires understanding that that work may be challenging and riddled with setbacks precisely because leaders are doing it right.

Researchers who do study central offices tend to do so in silos: zooming in on principal supervision or central office leadership of math reforms or the implementation of Title I and other federal policies. But studying central office transformation for equitable teaching and learning requires researchers to take institutional shifts across the central office as their main unit of analysis and to follow the reforms as they unfold over time at different paces and in various ways across units. How might researchers step outside their own silos to build better knowledge of central offices as a whole?

Given the centrality of new designs to central office transformation, we especially encourage scholars who conduct design-based research to consider that question. However, as we note in chapter 1, traditional design methods derived from classroom and other discrete settings may be a poor fit for supporting central office transformation for equitable teaching and learning and generating knowledge about it. We have seen district leaders use variations on those methods in ways that reinforced traditional silos and ultimately surfaced seemingly endless lists of problems of practice to address. How might researchers and district leaders collaborate using design methods that help them tackle inequities at their cross-cutting institutional roots within central offices? Such methods would focus participants on the premises that drive their current systems and on using research and other resources to forge new premises with equity at their core.

Taking next steps ultimately requires educational leaders across sectors and roles to resist becoming overwhelmed by the inherent challenges of supporting truly fundamental systemic change for equity. There could always be a better or potentially easier time to initiate such change. But as we have underscored, it's never the wrong time to do the right work.

Note on Methodology

The data we share in this book come from three rigorous empirical investigations we conducted in ten school districts ranging in size from rural districts with approximately 2,000 students to a 200,000-student subdistrict of a major urban school system (see table N.1). As we discussed in the introduction, we selected these districts mainly because leaders in each site indicated that they understood the fundamental mismatch between their long-standing central office work and what supporting districtwide equitable teaching and learning required. They all aimed to fundamentally and systemically transform their entire central office to drive equitable teaching and learning, and they invested significant time and other resources in those efforts in ways that bode well for their success.

DATA SOURCES

Given the complexity of central office transformation and the limitations of interviews and other self-report data for understanding such change processes, we relied on real-time observations as our main data source across studies. Between 2007 and 2021, over a total of four years, we spent almost 1,000 hours directly observing leaders as they designed and implemented central office transformation. Our observations included formal and informal central office staff meetings, myriad professional development sessions, and school board

TABLE N.1 District demographics during study periods

DISTRICT	APPROXIMATE NUMBER OF STUDENTS	PERCENTAGE OF STUDENTS IDENTIFYING AS BLACK, INDIGENOUS, LATINX, OR OF COLOR	COMMUNITY TYPE
1	200,000	83	Urban
2	49,000	86	Urban
3	48,000	43	Urban
4	46,000	89	Urban
5	19,000	82	Suburban
6	18,000	50	Suburban
7	5,000	36	Rural
8	3,000	15	Rural
9	2,000	15	Rural
10	2,000	20	Rural

hearings. We also shadowed central office leaders and staff members as they went about their daily work.

To ensure that we captured central office work as it unfolded, when observing, we either took verbatim notes in real time or audio-recorded discussions that we had professionally transcribed and carefully cleaned. We also created low-inference descriptions of other aspects of meetings such as late arrivals, facial expressions, and tone of voice.

We supplemented the observations with over 400 semistructured interviews with key actors in central office transformation, including superintendents, cabinet members, other central office leaders and staff members, school principals, and outside coaches. During the interviews, most of which lasted between sixty and seventy-five minutes, we probed for people's views of long-standing ways of working in their central offices and the design and implementation of central office transformation. We typically interviewed respondents more than once to capture any shifts in their understanding or perspectives over time. Through our research and other partnerships with districts, we also had conversations with central office leaders and staff members about central office transformation. When possible, we audio-recorded and transcribed those exchanges, totaling approximately 320 conversation hours.

We also collected and reviewed several hundred documents from each district that revealed the design, implementation, and evolution of central office transformation. Those documents included formal policies, employee handbooks, scorecards (as discussed in chapter 5), professional growth plans, school improvement protocols, agendas and other materials from professional development sessions, and public and private emails that respondents chose to share with us.

DATA ANALYSIS

We used NVivo software to analyze our data from each study through several common stages. First, we coded our data into low-inference categories such as month/year, central office unit, and professional position of meeting participant or respondent. That basic sorting of data was an important first step to help us examine the design and implementation of transformation within and across units and positions and over time.

Second, we went into our data by code to look for patterns in the problems that leaders aimed to solve with transformation generally and within specific units, their transformation designs or plans, and how they actually executed transformation in practice over time. We used the conceptual frameworks from our studies to ground this process. For example, for our analysis of principal supervision, our conceptual framework derived from sociocultural learning theory prompted us to code for instances of teaching-and-learning moves like "modeling" and "challenging talk" as well as examples of traditional principal supervision. Throughout the process, we triangulated across respondents and data sources, holding ourselves to the high standard of substantiating each reported finding with at least three different data points across respondents, sources, or both.

Third, we examined the findings we identified in the second step for any common premises they reflected. For example, not all districts redesigned their school improvement planning process as a main strategy to help teachers lead their own learning, but most executed some strategy consistent with that premise. We reported only those premises we could support with robust extant research connecting those premises with improved support for equitable teaching and learning, our or district's own outcomes data, or both. In our reports of findings in this book, we also share a few examples from our partnerships with districts across the country when those examples closely illustrate findings we already substantiated with our data using the methods noted here.

Our methods do not allow us to claim that particular premises or enactments of those premises *caused* improved equitable teaching and learning. Especially given the historical institutional embeddedness of racism and other inequities in school systems, we did not expect to see such improvements within the two- to three-year time frame of each study. Nor do available methods allow us to connect daily central office work directly to classroom teaching at the level of detail we achieve in our research. However, the consistency of our findings with robust extant research from sociocultural learning theory and other sources, as noted throughout this book, lends strong support for the associations we draw between the premises/enactments and improved support for equitable teaching and learning in the form of leading indicators such as principals' engagement in instructional leadership.

ABOUT THE VIGNETTES

The vignettes that start the introduction and most of the chapters are composite pictures we created based on our data to depict the experience of a school principal operating in a district whose central office work reflected all the new premises we share in each chapter. No one district was as far along with implementation of all the premises as described in each vignette, but we constructed the vignettes as illustrations of all the premises in one setting to help readers see the big picture—how all the premises worked together to support equitable teaching and learning. We developed the quotes in the vignettes by combining and streamlining central office leaders' actual statements.

Notes

Introduction

1. All formal names are pseudonyms. The vignettes are composite portraits of the main research findings elaborated in each chapter that we constructed for illustrative and teaching purposes. The events and quotes are consistent with, but not directly from, our data. For more on how we constructed these vignettes, please see the note on methodology.

2. Bryan McKinley Jones Brayboy, Angelina E. Castagno, and Emma Maughan, "Equality and Justice for All? Examining Race in Education Scholarship," *Review of Research in Education* 31, no. 1 (2007): 159–194; Sonya Douglass Horsford, "When Race Enters the Room: Improving Leadership and Learning Through Racial Literacy," *Theory Into Practice* 53, no. 2 (2014): 123–130; Gloria Ladson-Billings, "Just What Is Critical Race Theory, and What's It Doing in a Nice Field Like Education?," *International Journal of Qualitative Studies in Education* 11, no. 1 (1998): 7–24; Gerardo R. López, "The (Racially Neutral) Politics of Education: A Critical Race Theory Perspective," *Educational Administration Quarterly* 39, no. 1 (2003): 68–94; Richard H. Milner IV, "Critical Race Theory and Interest Convergence as Analytic Tools in Teacher Education Policies and Practices," *Journal of Teacher Education* 59, no. 4 (2008): 332–346; Iris Rotberg, "Crossroads: Integration and Segregation in Suburban School Districts," *Phi Delta Kappan* 101, no. 5 (2020): 44–49; Edward Taylor, "A Primer on Critical Race Theory: Who Are the Critical Race Theorists and What Are They Saying?," *Journal of Blacks in Higher Education* 19 (1998): 122; Edward Taylor, "The Foundations of Critical Race Theory in Education: An Introduction," in *Foundations of Critical Race Theory in Education,* ed. Edward Taylor et al. (New York: Routledge, 2009), 1–13.

3. Andrew Croft, Jane G. Coggshall, Megan Dolan, and Elizabeth Powers, "Job-Embedded Professional Development: What It Is, Who Is Responsible, and How to Get It Done Well," Issue Brief (Washington, DC: National Comprehensive Center for Teacher Quality, 2010); Linda Darling-Hammond et al., *Educator Supply, Demand, and Quality in North Carolina: Current Status and Recommendations* (Palo Alto, CA: Learning Policy Institute, 2017); Pamela Grossman, Samuel Wineburg, and Stephen Woolworth, "Toward a Theory of Teacher Community," *Teachers College Record* 103, no. 6 (2001): 942–1012. See also Jean Lave, "The Culture of Acquisition and the Practice of Understanding," in *Situated Cognition: Social, Semiotic, and Psychological Perspectives*, ed. David Kirshner and James A. Whitson (Mahwah, NJ: Lawrence Erlbaum & Associates, 1997), 63–82; Barbara Rogoff, "Developing Understanding of the Idea of Communities of Learners," *Mind, Culture, and Activity* 1, no. 4 (1994): 209–229; Roland G. Tharp and Ronald Gallimore, *Rousing Minds to Life: Teaching, Learning, and Schooling in Social Context* (Cambridge: Cambridge University Press, 1991); Etienne Wenger, "Communities of Practice: Learning as a Social System," *Systems Thinker* 9, no. 5 (1998): 2–3.
4. Samy H. Alim, Django Paris, and Casey Philip Wong, "Culturally Sustaining Pedagogy: A Critical Framework for Centering Communities," in *Handbook of the Cultural Foundations of Learning*, ed. Na'ilah Suad Nasir et al. (New York: Routledge, 2020), 261–276; Tyrone C. Howard and Andrea C. Rodriguez-Minkoff, "Culturally Relevant Pedagogy 20 Years Later: Progress or Pontificating? What Have We Learned, and Where Do We Go?," *Teachers College Record* 119, no. 1 (2017): 1–32; Gloria Ladson-Billings, "But That's Just Good Teaching! The Case for Culturally Relevant Pedagogy," *Theory Into Practice* 34, no. 3 (1995): 159–165.
5. John Seely Brown, Allan Collins, and Paul Duguid, "Situated Cognition and the Culture of Learning," *Educational Researcher* 18, no. 1 (1989): 32–42; Allan Collins, John Seely Brown, and Ann Holum, "Cognitive Apprenticeship: Making Thinking Visible," *American Educator* 15, no. 3 (1991): 6–11; Tharp and Gallimore, *Rousing Minds to Life*.

Chapter 1

1. Samy H. Alim, Django Paris, and Casey Philip Wong, "Culturally Sustaining Pedagogy: A Critical Framework for Centering Communities," in *Handbook of the Cultural Foundations of Learning*, ed. Na'ilah Suad Nasir et al. (New York: Routledge, 2020), 261–276; James A. Banks, *An Introduction to Multicultural Education*, 6th ed. (Seattle: University of Washington, 2019); Geneva Gay, *Culturally Responsive Teaching: Theory, Research, and Practice*, 3rd ed. (New York: Teachers College Press, 2018); Gloria Ladson-Billings, "But That's Just Good Teaching! The Case for

Culturally Relevant Pedagogy," *Theory Into Practice* 34, no. 3 (1995): 159–165; Gloria Ladson-Billings, *The Dreamkeepers: Successful Teachers of African American Children* (San Francisco: John Wiley, 2022); Gloria Ladson-Billings, "Culturally Relevant Pedagogy 2.0: AKA the Remix," *Harvard Educational Review* 84, no. 1 (2014): 74–84.

2. Jeni L. Burnette, Ernest H. O'Boyle, Eric M. Van Epps, Jeffrey M. Pollack, and Eli J. Finkel, "Mind-Sets Matter: A Meta-Analytic Review of Implicit Theories and Self-Regulation," *Psychological Bulletin* 139, no. 3 (2013): 655; Linda Darling-Hammond et al., *Educator Supply, Demand, and Quality in North Carolina: Current Status and Recommendations* (Palo Alto, CA: Learning Policy Institute, 2017); Pamela Grossman, Sarah Kavanagh, and P. C. Dean, "The Turn Towards Practice in Teacher Education," in *Teaching Core Practices in Teacher Education*, ed. Pamela Grossman (Cambridge, MA: Harvard Education Press, 2018), 1–14; Ladson-Billings, "Culturally Relevant Pedagogy 2.0."

3. John D. Bransford, Ann L. Brown, and Rodney R. Cocking, *How People Learn* (Washington, DC: National Academy Press, 2000); James G. Greeno, Allan M. Collins, and Lauren B. Resnick, "Cognition and Learning," *Handbook of Educational Psychology* 77 (1996): 15–46; Kara J. Jackson, Emily C. Shahan, Lynsey K. Gibbons, and Paul A. Cobb, "Launching Complex Tasks," *Mathematics Teaching in the Middle School* 18, no. 1 (2012): 24–29; James Pellegrino and Margaret Hilton, *Education for Life and Work: Developing Transferable Knowledge and Skills in the 21st Century* (Washington DC: National Research Council, 2012); Melissa Sommerfeld Gresalfi and Paul Cobb, "Cultivating Students' Discipline-Specific Dispositions as a Critical Goal for Pedagogy and Equity," *Pedagogies* 1, no. 1 (2006): 49–57.

4. Elham Kazemi and Deborah Stipek, "Promoting Conceptual Thinking in Four Upper-Elementary Mathematics Classrooms," *Journal of Education* 189, no. 1–2 (2009): 123–137; Elham Kazemi et al., "Math Labs: Teachers, Teacher Educators, and School Leaders Learning Together with and from Their Own Students," *Journal of Mathematics Education Leadership* 19, no. 1 (2018): 23–36; Morva McDonald, Elham Kazemi, and Sarah Schneider Kavanagh, "Core Practices and Pedagogies of Teacher Education: A Call for a Common Language and Collective Activity," *Journal of Teacher Education* 64, no. 5 (2013): 378–386; David Scott Yeager, Kali H. Trzesniewski, and Carol S. Dweck, "An Implicit Theories of Personality Intervention Reduces Adolescent Aggression in Response to Victimization and Exclusion," *Child Development* 84, no. 3 (2013): 970–988; David S. Yeager et al., "Boring but Important: A Self-Transcendent Purpose for Learning Fosters Academic Self-Regulation," *Journal of Personality and Social Psychology* 107, no. 4 (2014): 559–580.

5. Alim, Paris, and Wong, "Culturally Sustaining Pedagogy"; Cristina Viviana Groeger, *The Education Trap: Schools and the Remaking of Inequality in Boston* (Boston: Harvard University Press, 2021).

6. Django Paris and Samy H. Alim, "What Is Culturally Sustaining Pedagogy and Why Does It Matter?," in *Culturally Sustaining Pedagogies: Teaching and Learning for Justice in a Changing World*, ed. Django Paris and Samy H. Alim (New York: Teachers College Press, 2017); Gay, *Culturally Responsive Teaching*; Tyrone C. Howard and Andrea C. Rodriguez-Minkoff, "Culturally Relevant Pedagogy 20 Years Later: Progress or Pontificating? What Have We Learned, and Where Do We Go?," *Teachers College Record* 119, no. 1 (2017): 1–32; David E. Kirkland, "Urban Literacy Learning," in *Handbook of Urban Education*, ed. Richard Milner and Kofi Lomotey (Philadelphia: Routledge, 2013), 432–450; Ladson-Billings, "Culturally Relevant Pedagogy 2.0"; Zeus Leonardo, *Race, Whiteness, and Education* (Philadelphia: Routledge, 2009).

7. Gloria Ladson-Billings, "What We Can Learn from Multicultural Education Research," *Educational Leadership* 51, no. 8 (1994): 22–26; Ladson-Billings, *The Dreamkeepers*. See also Luis C. Moll and Norma Gonzalez, "Lessons from Research with Language-Minority Children," *Journal of Reading Behavior* 26, no. 4 (1994): 439–456; Ivory A. Toldson, *No BS (Bad Stats)* (Leiden, Netherlands: Brill, 2019).

8. Eve Tuck, "Suspending Damage: A Letter to Communities," *Harvard Educational Review* 79, no. 3 (2009): 409–428.

9. Alim, Paris, and Wong, "Culturally Sustaining Pedagogy"; Sarah Diem and Anjalé D. Welton, *Anti-Racist Educational Leadership and Policy: Addressing Racism in Public Education* (Oxfordshire, UK: Routledge, 2020); Ladson-Billings, "Culturally Relevant Pedagogy 2.0."

10. Alim, Paris, and Wong, "Culturally Sustaining Pedagogy"; Howard and Rodriguez-Minkoff, "Culturally Relevant Pedagogy 20 Years Later"; Ladson-Billings, "Culturally Relevant Pedagogy 2.0."

11. Alim, Paris, and Wong, "Culturally Sustaining Pedagogy"; Gay, *Culturally Responsive Teaching*; Howard and Rodriguez-Minkoff, "Culturally Relevant Pedagogy 20 Years Later"; Ladson-Billings, "But That's Just Good Teaching!"; Tuck, "Suspending Damage."

12. Gregory F. Branch, Eric A. Hanushek, and Steven G. Rivkin, *Estimating the Effect of Leaders on Public Sector Productivity: The Case of School Principals* (Cambridge, MA: National Bureau of Economic Research, 2012); Ellen Goldring et al., "Make Room Value Added: Principals' Human Capital Decisions and the Emergence of Teacher Observation Data," *Educational Researcher* 44, no. 2 (2015): 96–104; Jason A. Grissom, Anna J. Egalite, and Constance A. Lindsay, *How Principals Affect Students and Schools* (New York: Wallace Foundation, 2021); Kenneth Leithwood, Karen Seashore Louis, Stephen Anderson, and Kyla Wahlstrom, *Review of Research: How*

Leadership Influences Student Learning (New York: Wallace Foundation, 2004); Helen M. Marks and Susan M. Printy, "Principal Leadership and School Performance: An Integration of Transformational and Instructional Leadership," *Educational Administration Quarterly* 39, no. 3 (2003): 370–397; Christine M. Neumerski, "Rethinking Instructional Leadership, A Review: What Do We Know About Principal, Teacher, and Coach Instructional Leadership, and Where Should We Go From Here?," *Educational Administration Quarterly* 49, no. 2 (2013): 310–347.

13. Joseph Blase and Jo Blase, "Principals' Instructional Leadership and Teacher Development: Teachers' Perspectives," *Educational Administration Quarterly* 35, no. 3 (1999): 349–378; Roger Goddard, Yvonne Goddard, Eun Sook Kim, and Robert Miller, "A Theoretical and Empirical Analysis of the Roles of Instructional Leadership, Teacher Collaboration, and Collective Efficacy Beliefs in Support of Student Learning," *American Journal of Education* 121, no. 4 (2015): 501–530; Marks and Printy, "Principal Leadership and School Performance"; Robert J. Miller and Brian Rowan, "Effects of Organic Management on Student Achievement," *American Educational Research Journal* 43, no. 2 (2006): 219–253; William M. Saunders, Claude N. Goldenberg, and Ronald Gallimore, "Increasing Achievement by Focusing Grade-Level Teams on Improving Classroom Learning: A Prospective, Quasi-Experimental Study of Title I Schools," *American Educational Research Journal* 46, no. 4 (2009): 1006–1033; Elizabeth Leisy Stosich, Candice Bocala, and Michelle Forman, "Building Coherence for Instructional Improvement Through Professional Development: A Design-Based Implementation Research Study," *Educational Management Administration & Leadership* 46, no. 5 (2018): 864–880; George Theoharis, "Social Justice Educational Leaders and Resistance: Toward a Theory of Social Justice Leadership," *Educational Administration Quarterly* 43, no. 2 (2007): 221–258; Rose M. Ylimaki, Jeffrey V. Bennett, Jingjing Fan, and Elia Villasenor, "Notions of 'Success' in Southern Arizona Schools: Principal Leadership in Changing Demographic and Border Contexts," *Leadership and Policy in Schools* 11, no. 2 (2012): 168–193.

14. Cheryl Graczewski, Joel Knudson, and Deborah J. Holtzman, "Instructional Leadership in Practice: What Does It Look Like, and What Influence Does It Have?," *Journal of Education for Students Placed at Risk* 14, no. 1 (2009): 72–96; Jason A. Grissom, Demetra Kalogrides, and Susanna Loeb, "Using Student Test Scores to Measure Principal Performance," *Educational Evaluation and Policy Analysis* 37, no. 1 (2015): 3–28; Christine M. Neumerski et al., "Restructuring Instructional Leadership: How Multiple-Measure Teacher Evaluation Systems Are Redefining the Role of the School Principal," *Elementary School Journal* 119, no. 2 (2018): 270–297; Karen Seashore Louis et al., *Learning From Leadership: Investigating the Links to Improved Student Learning* (New York: Wallace Foundation, 2010).

15. Bradley W. Carpenter and Sarah Diem, "Guidance Matters: A Critical Discourse Analysis of the Race-Related Policy Vocabularies Shaping Leadership Preparation," *Urban Education* 50, no. 5 (2015): 515–534; Brent Davis, Dennis Sumara, and Rebecca Luce-Kapler, *Engaging Minds: Cultures of Education and Practices of Teaching* (Philadelphia: Routledge, 2015); Peter Demerath, "The Emotional Ecology of School Improvement Culture: Charged Meanings and Common Moral Purpose," *Journal of Educational Administration* 56, no. 5 (2018): 488–503; Mollie K. Galloway and Ann M. Ishimaru, "Radical Recentering: Equity in Educational Leadership Standards," *Educational Administration Quarterly* 51, no. 3 (2015): 372–408; Mollie K. Galloway and Ann M. Ishimaru, "Equitable Leadership on the Ground: Converging on High-Leverage Practices," *Education Policy Analysis Archives* 25 (2017): 1–36; Mollie K. Galloway and Ann M. Ishimaru, "Leading Equity Teams: The Role of Formal Leaders in Building Organizational Capacity for Equity," *Journal of Education for Students Placed at Risk* 25, no. 2 (2020): 107–125; Mark A. Gooden and Michael Dantley, "Centering Race in a Framework for Leadership Preparation," *Journal of Research on Leadership Education* 7, no. 2 (2012): 237–253; Muhammad A. Khalifa, Mark Anthony Gooden, and James Earl Davis, "Culturally Responsive School Leadership: A Synthesis of the Literature," *Review of Educational Research* 86, no. 4 (2016): 1272–1311; George Theoharis and Joanne O'Toole, "Leading Inclusive ELL: Social Justice Leadership for English Language Learners," *Educational Administration Quarterly* 47, no. 4 (2011): 646–688; Ylimaki et al., "Notions of 'Success' in Southern Arizona Schools."
16. Khalifa, Gooden, and Davis, "Culturally Responsive School Leadership"; George Theoharis and Marcelle Haddix, "Undermining Racism and a Whiteness Ideology: White Principals Living a Commitment to Equitable and Excellent Schools," *Urban Education* 46, no. 6 (2011): 1332–1351.
17. Sonya Douglass Horsford, "When Race Enters the Room: Improving Leadership and Learning Through Racial Literacy," *Theory Into Practice* 53, no. 2 (2014): 123–130; Sonya Douglass Horsford, Tanetha Grosland, and Kelly Morgan Gunn, "Pedagogy of the Personal and Professional: Toward a Framework for Culturally Relevant Leadership," *Journal of School Leadership* 21, no. 4 (2011): 582–606; Sharon I. Radd, Gretchen Givens Generett, Mark Anthony Gooden, and George Theoharis, *Five Practices for Equity-Focused School Leadership* (Alexandria, VA: ASCD, 2021).
18. Jason A. Grissom, "Can Good Principals Keep Teachers in Disadvantaged Schools? Linking Principal Effectiveness to Teacher Satisfaction and Turnover in Hard-to-Staff Environments," *Teachers College Record* 113, no. 11 (2011): 2552–2585; Julia Koppich and Connie Showalter, *Strategic Management of Human Capital: Cross-Case Analysis* (Philadelphia: Consortium for Policy Research in Education, 2008); Katherine Cumings

Mansfield and Gaëtane Jean-Marie, "Courageous Conversations About Race, Class, and Gender: Voices and Lessons from the Field," *International Journal of Qualitative Studies in Education* 28, no. 7 (2015): 819–841.

19. Jean Anyon, *Ghetto Schooling: A Political Economy of Urban Educational Reform* (New York: Teachers College Press, 1997).

20. James Wright, Ronald W. Whitaker, Muhammad Khalifa, and Felecia Briscoe, "The Color of Neoliberal Reform: A Critical Race Policy Analysis of School District Takeovers in Michigan," *Urban Education* 55, no. 3 (2020): 424–447. See also Muhammad A. Khalifa, Michael E. Jennings, Felecia Briscoe, Ashley M. Oleszweski, and Nimo Abdi, "Racism? Administrative and Community Perspectives in Data-Driven Decision Making: Systemic Perspectives Versus Technical-Rational Perspectives," *Urban Education* 49, no. 2 (2014): 147–181.

21. Bryan McKinley Jones Brayboy, Angelina E. Castagno, and Emma Maughan, "Equality and Justice for All? Examining Race in Education Scholarship," *Review of Research in Education* 31, no. 1 (2007): 159–194; Douglass Horsford, "When Race Enters the Room"; Khalifa, Gooden, and Davis, "Culturally Responsive School Leadership"; Gloria Ladson-Billings, "Just What Is Critical Race Theory, and What's It Doing in a Nice Field Like Education?," *International Journal of Qualitative Studies in Education* 11, no. 1 (1998): 7–24; Gerardo R. López, "The (Racially Neutral) Politics of Education: A Critical Race Theory Perspective," *Educational Administration Quarterly* 39, no. 1 (2003): 68–94; Richard H. Milner IV, "Critical Race Theory and Interest Convergence as Analytic Tools in Teacher Education Policies and Practices," *Journal of Teacher Education* 59, no. 4 (2008): 332–346; Iris Rotberg, "Crossroads: Integration and Segregation in Suburban School Districts," *Phi Delta Kappan* 101, no. 5 (2020): 44–49.

22. Paul J. DiMaggio and Walter W. Powell, "The Iron Cage Revisited: Institutional Isomorphism and Collective Rationality in Organizational Fields," *American Sociological Review* 48, no. 2 (1983): 147–160; Royston Greenwood and Christopher R. Hinings, "Understanding Radical Organizational Change: Bringing Together the Old and the New Institutionalism," *Academy of Management Review* 21, no. 4 (1996): 1022–1054; Anjalé D. Welton, Devean R. Owens, and Eboni M. Zamani-Gallaher, "Anti-Racist Change: A Conceptual Framework for Educational Institutions to Take Systemic Action," *Teachers College Record* 120, no. 14 (2018): 1–22.

23. Meredith I. Honig, "No Small Thing: School District Central Office Bureaucracies and the Implementation of New Small Autonomous Schools Initiatives," *American Educational Research Journal* 46, no. 2 (2009): 387–422; Meredith I. Honig and Lydia R. Rainey, *Supervising Principals for Instructional Leadership: A Teaching and Learning Approach* (Cambridge,

MA: Harvard Education Press, 2020); Meredith I. Honig and Nitya Venkateswaran, "School–Central Office Relationships in Evidence Use: Understanding Evidence Use as a Systems Problem," *American Journal of Education* 118, no. 2 (2012): 199–222.

24. Ladson-Billings, "Just What Is Critical Race Theory"; López, "The (Racially Neutral) Politics of Education"; Welton, Owens, and Zamani-Gallaher, "Anti-Racist Change."

25. H. Richard Milner IV, "Race, Culture, and Researcher Positionality: Working Through Dangers Seen, Unseen, and Unforeseen," *Educational Researcher* 36, no. 7 (2007): 388–400; James Joseph Scheurich and Michelle D. Young, "Coloring Epistemologies: Are Our Research Epistemologies Racially Biased?," *Educational Researcher* 26, no. 4 (1997): 4–16.

26. Khalifa et al., "Racism?"; Tina M. Trujillo, "The Politics of District Instructional Policy Formation: Compromising Equity and Rigor," *Educational Policy* 27, no. 3 (2013): 531–559; Welton, Owens, and Zamani-Gallaher, "Anti-Racist Change."

27. See, for example, Groeger, *The Education Trap*; Donald J. Peurach, David K. Cohen, and James P. Spillane, "Governments, Markets, and Instruction: Considerations for Cross-National Research," *Journal of Educational Administration* 54, no. 4 (2019): 393–410; David B. Tyack, *The One Best System: A History of American Urban Education* (Cambridge, MA: Harvard University Press, 1974).

28. David A. Gamson and Emily M. Hodge, "Education Research and the Shifting Landscape of the American School District, 1816 to 2016," *Review of Research in Education* 40, no. 1 (2016): 225. See also Lawrence A. Cremin, *Popular Education and Its Discontents* (New York: HarperCollins, 1990); Tyack, *The One Best System*; David B. Tyack and Larry Cuban, *Tinkering Toward Utopia: A Century of Public School Reform* (Cambridge, MA: Harvard University Press, 1995).

29. Jeffrey Mirel, *The Rise and Fall of an Urban School System: Detroit, 1907–81* (Ann Arbor: University of Michigan Press, 1999); Tracy L. Steffes, "Solving the 'Rural School Problem': New State Aid, Standards, and Supervision of Local Schools, 1900–1933," *History of Education Quarterly* 48, no. 2 (2008): 181–220.

30. Groeger, *The Education Trap*; Donald J. Peurach, David K. Cohen, Maxwell M. Yurkofsky, and James P. Spillane, "From Mass Schooling to Education Systems: Changing Patterns in the Organization and Management of Instruction," *Review of Research in Education* 43, no. 1 (2019): 32–67; Trujillo, "The Politics of District Instructional Policy Formation"; Tyack, *The One Best System*.

31. Groeger, *The Education Trap*; Herbert M. Kliebard, *Schooled to Work: Vocationalism and the American Curriculum, 1876–1946*, Reflective History Series (New York: Teachers College Press, 1999); Herbert M.

Kliebard, *The Struggle for the American Curriculum, 1893–1958* (Philadelphia: Routledge, 2004); Vanessa Siddle Walker, "Valued Segregated Schools for African American Children in the South, 1935–1969: A Review of Common Themes and Characteristics," *Review of Educational Research* 70, no. 3 (2000): 253–285.

32. Meredith I. Honig, "Complexity and Policy Implementation," in *New Directions in Education Policy Implementation: Confronting Complexity*, ed. Meredith I. Honig (Albany, NY: SUNY Press, 2006), 1–25; Allan Odden, ed., *Education Policy Implementation* (Albany, NY: SUNY Press, 1991); Sandra J. Stein, *The Culture of Education Policy* (New York: Teachers College Press, 2004).

33. Julia H. Kaufman and Melissa Kay Diliberti, *Divergent and Inequitable Teaching and Learning Pathways During (and Perhaps Beyond) the Pandemic: Key Findings from the American Educator Panels Spring 2021 COVID-19 Surveys* (Santa Monica, CA: RAND Corporation, 2021); Megan Kuhfeld et al., "Projecting the Potential Impact of COVID-19 School Closures on Academic Achievement," *Educational Researcher* 49, no. 8 (2020): 549–565; Mark Liberman, "Taking Attendance During Coronavirus Closures," *Education Week*, April 17, 2020.

34. Eliza Shapiro, Erica L. Greene, and Juliana Kim, "One Thing That's Missing in the Reopening Plans of US Schools: The Trust of Black Families," *New York Times*, February 1, 2021.

35. Tyack and Cuban, *Tinkering Toward Utopia*.

36. Honig, "No Small Thing"; Keith A. Nitta, Sharon L. Wrobel, Joseph Y. Howard, and Ellen Jimmerson-Eddings, "Leading Change of a School District Reorganization," *Public Performance & Management Review* 32, no. 3 (2009): 463–488.

37. Sean Cavanaugh, "What K–12 Officials Expect from Education Companies on Diversity, Equity, and Inclusion," *Education Week*, December 3, 2021; Linda Skrla, Kathryn Bell McKenzie, and James Joseph Scheurich, eds., *Using Equity Audits to Create Equitable and Excellent Schools* (Thousand Oaks, CA: Corwin, 2009); Sarah D. Sparks, "How Does An Equity Audit Work?," *Education Week*, September 17, 2015.

38. Jill Anderson, "Five Ways to Support Equity Leaders," *Usable Knowledge*, June 28, 2021; Decoteau J. Irby et al., *K–12 Equity Directors: Configuring the Role for Impact* (Chicago: Center for Urban Education Leadership, 2021); Mary Rice-Boothe, "So You Want to Hire—or Become—an Equity Officer?," *District Administrator*, February 2021; Mary Rice-Boothe, "What Equity Officers See as Their Challenges," *School Administrator*, November 2021; Merri Rosenberg, "New to the Table: The Chief Equity Officer," *School Administrator*, November 2021; Christina Samuels, "The Challenging, Often Isolating Work of School District Chief Equity Officers," *Education Week*, October 19, 2019.

39. Honig, "No Small Thing." See also Erika A. Patall, Harris Cooper, and Ashley Batts Allen, "Extending the School Day or School Year: A Systematic Review of Research (1985–2009)," *Review of Educational Research* 80, no. 3 (2010): 401–436; Charles M. Payne, *So Much Reform, So Little Change: The Persistence of Failure in Urban Schools* (Cambridge, MA: Harvard Education Press, 2008).

40. Irby et al., *K–12 Equity Directors*; Joshua P. Starr, "So You Hired an Equity Leader, Now What?," *Phi Delta Kappan*, February 18, 2020. See also Monica B. Vela, Monica Lypson, and William A. McDade, "Diversity, Equity, and Inclusion Officer Position Available: Proceed with Caution," *Journal of Graduate Medical Education* 13, no. 6 (2021): 771–773.

41. Sarah D. Sparks, "Training Bias Out of Teachers: Research Shows Little Promise So Far," *Education Week*, November 17, 2020.

42. Ebony N. Bridwell-Mitchell and David G. Sherer, "Institutional Complexity and Policy Implementation: How Underlying Logics Drive Teacher Interpretations of Reform," *Educational Evaluation and Policy Analysis* 39, no. 2 (2017): 223–247; James P. Spillane, "State Policy and the Nonmonolithic Nature of the Local School District: Organizational and Professional Considerations," *American Educational Research Journal* 35, no. 1 (1998): 33–63; James P. Spillane, "Cognition and Policy Implementation: District Policymakers and the Reform of Mathematics Education," *Cognition and Instruction* 18, no. 2 (2000): 141–179; James P. Spillane, *Standards Deviation: How Schools Misunderstand Education Policy* (Cambridge, MA: Harvard University Press, 2009); James P. Spillane, Brian J. Reiser, and Todd Reimer, "Policy Implementation and Cognition: Reframing and Refocusing Implementation Research," *Review of Educational Research* 72, no. 3 (2002): 387–431.

43. Meredith I. Honig, "Building Policy from Practice: District Central Office Administrators' Roles and Capacity for Implementing Collaborative Education Policy," *Educational Administration Quarterly* 39, no. 3 (2003): 292–338.

44. IDEO, *Design Thinking for Educators*, 2nd ed. (Palo Alto, CA: IDEO, 2011); Anthony Bryk et al., *Learning to Improve: How America's Schools Can Get Better at Getting Better* (Cambridge, MA: Harvard Education Press, 2015); Anthony S. Bryk, *Improvement in Action: Advancing Quality in America's Schools* (Cambridge, MA: Harvard Education Press, 2020); Barry J. Fishman et al., "Design-Based Implementation Research: An Emerging Model for Transforming the Relationship of Research and Practice," *Teachers College Record* 115, no. 14 (2013): 136–156; William R. Penuel et al., "Organizing Research and Development at the Intersection of Learning, Implementation, and Design," *Educational Researcher* 40, no. 7 (2011): 331–337.

45. Honig and Rainey, *Supervising Principals for Instructional Leadership*.

46. Yrjö Engeström, Juhana Rantavuori, and Hannele Kerosuo, "Expansive Learning in a Library: Actions, Cycles and Deviations from Instructional Intentions," *Vocations and Learning* 6, no. 1 (2013): 81–106; Meredith I. Honig, "Beyond the Policy Memo: Designing to Strengthen the Practice of District Central Office Leadership for Instructional Improvement at Scale," *Teachers College Record* 115, no. 14 (2013): 256–273; D. Kevin O'Neill, "Understanding Design Research–Practice Partnerships in Context and Time: Why Learning Sciences Scholars Should Learn from Cultural-Historical Activity Theory Approaches to Design-Based Research," *Journal of the Learning Sciences* 25, no. 4 (2016): 497–502.

Chapter 2

1. These units go by various names in districts across the country, including Curriculum and Instruction and Academics.
2. The people in charge of Teaching and Learning varied in their titles, which included associate superintendent, assistant superintendent, chief academic officer, and executive director. In very small districts, superintendents serve in those roles. Consistent with our confidentiality agreements with our study participants, here we refer to people in those roles generally as "director."
3. Allan Collins, John Seely Brown, and Ann Holum, "Cognitive Apprenticeship: Making Thinking Visible," *American Educator* 15, no. 3 (1991): 6–11; Allan Collins, John Seely Brown, and Ann Holum, *Cognitive Apprenticeship: Making Thinking Visible. The Principles of Learning: Study Tools for Educators* (Pittsburgh, PA: University of Pittsburgh, 2003); K. Anders Ericsson, "Deliberate Practice and the Acquisition and Maintenance of Expert Performance in Medicine and Related Domains," *Academic Medicine* 79, no. 10 (2004): S70–S81; K. Anders Ericsson, "The Influence of Experience and Deliberate Practice on the Development of Superior Expert Performance," in *The Cambridge Handbook of Expertise and Expert Performance*, Cambridge Handbooks in Psychology, ed. K. Anders Ericsson, Neil Charness, Paul J. Feltovich, and Robert R. Hoffman (Cambridge: Cambridge University Press, 2006), 683–704; Peter Smagorinsky, Leslie Susan Cook, and Tara Star Johnson, "The Twisting Path of Concept Development in Learning to Teach," *Teachers College Record* 105, no. 8 (2003): 1399–1436.
4. Ericsson, "Deliberate Practice"; Ericsson, "The Influence of Experience"; Barbara Rogoff, Jacqueline Baker-Sennett, Pilar Lacasa, and Denise Goldsmith, "Development Through Participation in Sociocultural Activity," *New Directions for Child and Adolescent Development* 1995, no. 67 (1995): 45–65; Etienne Wenger, *Communities of Practice: Learning, Meaning, and Identity* (Cambridge: Cambridge University Press, 1999).
5. John Seely Brown, Allan Collins, and Paul Duguid, "Situated Cognition and the Culture of Learning," *Educational Researcher* 18, no. 1 (1989): 32–42;

Barbara Rogoff, "Developing Understanding of the Idea of Communities of Learners," *Mind, Culture, and Activity* 1, no. 4 (1994): 209–229; Rogoff et al., "Development Through Participation"; Wenger, *Communities of Practice*.

6. John D. Bransford, Ann L. Brown, and Rodney R. Cocking, *How People Learn* (Washington, DC: National Academy Press, 2000); Angela Calabrese Barton and Edna Tan, "We Be Burnin'! Agency, Identity, and Science Learning," *Journal of the Learning Sciences* 19, no. 2 (2010): 187–229; Barbara Rogoff et al., "Firsthand Learning Through Intent Participation," *Annual Review of Psychology* 54, no. 1 (2003): 175–203; Roland G. Tharp and Ronald Gallimore, *Rousing Minds to Life: Teaching, Learning, and Schooling in Social Context* (Cambridge: Cambridge University Press, 1991).

7. Albert Bandura, "Exercise of Human Agency Through Collective Efficacy," *Current Directions in Psychological Science* 9, no. 3 (2000): 75–78; Albert Bandura, "Social Cognitive Theory: An Agentic Perspective," *Annual Review of Psychology* 52, no. 1 (2001): 1–26; Bransford, Brown, and Cocking, *How People Learn*.

8. Brown, Collins, and Duguid, "Situated Cognition"; Rogoff et al., "Development Through Participation"; Tharp and Gallimore, *Rousing Minds to Life*.

9. John Seely Brown, "Research That Reinvents the Corporation," *Harvard Business Review* 69, no. 1 (1991): 102–110; Brown, Collins, and Duguid, "Situated Cognition"; Andrew Croft et al., *Job-Embedded Professional Development: What It Is, Who Is Responsible, and How to Get It Done Well* (Washington, DC: National Comprehensive Center for Teacher Quality, 2010); James G. Greeno, Allan M. Collins, and Lauren B. Resnick, "Cognition and Learning," in *Handbook of Educational Psychology*, ed. David C. Berliner and Robert C. Calfee (New York: Macmillan, 1996), 15–46; Jean Lave and Etienne Wenger, *Situated Learning: Legitimate Peripheral Participation* (Cambridge: Cambridge University Press, 1991); Barbara Rogoff, *Apprenticeship in Thinking: Cognitive Development in Social Context* (Oxford: Oxford University Press, 1990); Barbara Rogoff et al., "Firsthand Learning Through Intent Participation," *Annual Review of Psychology* 54, no. 1 (2003): 175–203.

10. Brown, "Research That Reinvents the Corporation"; Jean Lave, "Teaching, as Learning, in Practice," *Mind, Culture, and Activity* 3, no. 3 (1996): 149–164; Lave and Wenger, *Situated Learning*; Rogoff, "Developing Understanding"; Wenger, *Communities of Practice*.

11. Sanne F. Akkerman and Arthur Bakker, "Boundary Crossing and Boundary Objects," *Review of Educational Research* 81, no. 2 (2011): 132–169; John Seely Brown and Paul Duguid, "Organizing Knowledge," *California Management Review* 40, no. 3 (1998): 90–111; Yrjö Engeström, "Objects, Contradictions and Collaboration in Medical Cognition: An

Activity-Theoretical Perspective," *Artificial Intelligence in Medicine* 7, no. 5 (1995): 395–412; Yrjö Engeström, "Expansive Learning at Work: Toward an Activity Theoretical Reconceptualization," *Journal of Education and Work* 14, no. 1 (2001): 133–156; Wenger, *Communities of Practice*.

12. Rogoff et al., "Development Through Participation"; Wenger, *Communities of Practice*.

13. Akkerman and Bakker, "Boundary Crossing"; Sanne Akkerman and Ton Bruining, "Multilevel Boundary Crossing in a Professional Development School Partnership," *Journal of the Learning Sciences* 25, no. 2 (2016): 240–284; Paul Cobb and Janet Bowers, "Cognitive and Situated Learning Perspectives in Theory and Practice," *Educational Researcher* 28, no. 2 (1999): 4–15; Wenger, *Communities of Practice*.

14. Tharp and Gallimore, *Rousing Minds to Life*.

15. Bransford, Brown, and Cocking, *How People Learn*; Ericsson, "Deliberate Practice"; Ericsson, "The Influence of Experience." See also Carol Ann Tomlinson, *The Differentiated Classroom: Responding to the Needs of All Learners* (Washington, DC: ASCD, 2014).

16. Ericsson, "Deliberate Practice"; Ericsson, "The Influence of Experience"; Roy D. Pea, "The Social and Technological Dimensions of Scaffolding and Related Theoretical Concepts for Learning, Education, and Human Activity," *Journal of the Learning Sciences* 13, no. 3 (2004): 423–451.

Chapter 3

1. Herbert G. Heneman III and Anthony T. Milanowski, *Assessing Human Resource Alignment: The Foundation for Building Total Teacher Quality Improvement* (Madison, WI: Consortium for Policy Research in Education, 2007); Allen Odden and J. A. Kelley, *What Is SMHC? Strategic Management of Human Capital Project of the Consortium for Policy Research in Education* (Madison: Wisconsin Center for Education Research, University of Wisconsin–Madison, 2008); Margaret L. Plecki et al., *How Leaders Invest Staffing Resources for Learning Improvement* (Seattle: University of Washington Center for the Study of Teaching and Policy, 2010); Mark A. Smylie, Debra Miretzky, and Pamela Konkol, "Rethinking Teacher Workforce Development: A Strategic Human Resource Management Perspective," *Teachers College Record* 106, no. 13 (2004): 34–69; Judy Wurtzel and Rachel Curtis, *Human Capital Framework for K–12 Urban Education: Organizing for Success* (Washington, DC: Aspen Institute, 2008).

2. Heneman and Milanowski, *Assessing Human Resource Alignment*.

3. Heneman and Milanowski, *Assessing Human Resource Alignment*.

4. Plecki et al., *How Leaders Invest Staffing Resources for Learning Improvement*; Rachel E. Curtis and Judy Wurtzel, *Teaching Talent: A Visionary Framework for Human Capital in Education* (Cambridge, MA: Harvard Education Press, 2010).

5. Ramon B. Goings, Larry J. Walker, and Keah L. Wade, "The Influence of Intuition on Human Resource Officers' Perspectives on Hiring Teachers of Color," *Journal of School Leadership* 31, no. 3 (2021): 189–208.

6. Inge Bakkenes, Jan D. Vermunt, and Theo Wubbels, "Teacher Learning in the Context of Educational Innovation: Learning Activities and Learning Outcomes of Experienced Teachers," *Learning and Instruction* 20, no. 6 (2010): 533–548; Jean Lave, "Teaching, as Learning, in Practice," *Mind, Culture, and Activity* 3, no. 3 (1996): 149–164; Jean Lave and Etienne Wenger, *Situated Learning: Legitimate Peripheral Participation* (Cambridge: Cambridge University Press, 1991); Barbara Rogoff, "Developing Understanding of the Idea of Communities of Learners," *Mind, Culture, and Activity* 1, no. 4 (1994): 209–229; Barbara Rogoff, Jacqueline Baker-Sennett, Pilar Lacasa, and Denise Goldsmith, "Development Through Participation in Sociocultural Activity," *New Directions for Child and Adolescent Development* 1995, no. 67 (1995): 45–65; Etienne Wenger, *Communities of Practice: Learning, Meaning, and Identity* (Cambridge: Cambridge University Press, 1999).

7. John D. Bransford, Ann L. Brown, and Rodney R. Cocking, *How People Learn* (Washington, DC: National Academy Press, 2000); Lave and Wenger, *Situated Learning*; Wenger, *Communities of Practice*.

8. Betty Achinstein et al., "Retaining Teachers of Color: A Pressing Problem and a Potential Strategy for 'Hard-to-Staff' Schools," *Review of Educational Research* 80, no. 1 (2010): 71–107; Davis Dixon, Ashley Griffin, and Mark Teoh, *If You Listen, We Will Stay: Why Teachers of Color Leave and How to Disrupt Teacher Turnover* (Washington, DC: Education Trust, 2019); Richard Ingersoll, Henry May, and Gregory Collins, "Recruitment, Employment, Retention and the Minority Teacher Shortage," *Education Policy Analysis Archives* 27, no. 37 (2019); Rita Kohli, "Lessons for Teacher Education: The Role of Critical Professional Development in Teacher of Color Retention," *Journal of Teacher Education* 70, no. 1 (2019): 39–50.

9. Jason A. Grissom, Luis A. Rodriguez, and Emily C. Kern, "Teacher and Principal Diversity and the Representation of Students of Color in Gifted Programs: Evidence from National Data," *Elementary School Journal* 117, no. 3 (2017): 396–422; Edward Liu and Susan Moore Johnson, "New Teachers' Experiences of Hiring: Late, Rushed, and Information-Poor," *Educational Administration Quarterly* 42, no. 3 (2006): 324–360; Piety Runhaar, "How Can Schools and Teachers Benefit from Human Resources Management? Conceptualising HRM from Content and Process Perspectives," *Educational Management Administration & Leadership* 45, no. 4 (2017): 639–656.

Chapter 4

1. We adapted this vignette and the main content of this chapter from our book: Meredith I. Honig and Lydia R. Rainey, *Supervising Principals for Instructional Leadership: A Teaching and Learning Approach* (Cambridge, MA: Harvard Education Press, 2020).

2. In other chapters, the examples in the "limitations" section come from leaders' reports of their central office prior to central office transformation. The claims in this section also reflect leaders' reports, but most of the examples come from our own observations of principal supervision during central office transformation that still reflected the traditional approach leaders were trying to move away from. We took that different approach in this chapter because we viewed our observational data as a more robust source of evidence of practice than self-reports.

3. For a detailed discussion of our methods regarding principal supervisors, please see Honig and Rainey, *Supervising Principals for Instructional Leadership*.

4. Allan Collins, John Seely Brown, and Ann Holum, *Cognitive Apprenticeship: Making Thinking Visible. The Principles of Learning: Study Tools for Educators* (Pittsburgh, PA: University of Pittsburgh, 2003); Allan Collins, John Seely Brown, and Ann Holum, "Cognitive Apprenticeship: Making Thinking Visible," *American Educator* 15, no. 3 (1991): 6–11; K. Anders Ericsson, "Deliberate Practice and the Acquisition and Maintenance of Expert Performance in Medicine and Related Domains," *Academic Medicine* 79, no. 10 (2004): S70–S81; K. Anders Ericsson, "The Influence of Experience and Deliberate Practice on the Development of Superior Expert Performance," in *The Cambridge Handbook of Expertise and Expert Performance*, Cambridge Handbooks in Psychology, ed. K. Anders Ericsson, Neil Charness, Paul J. Feltovich, and Robert R. Hoffman (Cambridge: Cambridge University Press, 2006), 683–704; Peter Smagorinsky, Leslie Susan Cook, and Tara Star Johnson, "The Twisting Path of Concept Development in Learning to Teach," *Teachers College Record* 105, no. 8 (2003): 1399–1436.

5. John Seely Brown, Allan Collins, and Paul Duguid, "Situated Cognition and the Culture of Learning," *Educational Researcher* 18, no. 1 (1989): 32–42; Ericsson, "Deliberate Practice"; Ericsson, "The Influence of Experience"; Barbara Rogoff, "Developing Understanding of the Idea of Communities of Learners," *Mind, Culture, and Activity* 1, no. 4 (1994): 209–229; Barbara Rogoff, Jacqueline Baker-Sennett, Pilar Lacasa, and Denise Goldsmith, "Development Through Participation in Sociocultural Activity," *New Directions for Child and Adolescent Development* 1995, no. 67 (1995): 45–65; Etienne Wenger, *Communities of Practice: Learning, Meaning, and Identity* (Cambridge: Cambridge University Press, 1999).

6. Barbara Rogoff et al., "Firsthand Learning Through Intent Participation," *Annual Review of Psychology* 54, no. 1 (2003): 175–203; Angela Calabrese Barton and Edna Tan, "We Be Burnin'! Agency, Identity, and Science Learning," *Journal of the Learning Sciences* 19, no. 2 (2010): 187–229.

7. John D. Bransford, Ann L. Brown, and Rodney R. Cocking, *How People Learn* (Washington, DC: National Academy Press, 2000); Albert Bandura, "Social Cognitive Theory: An Agentic Perspective," *Annual Review of Psychology* 52, no. 1 (2001): 1–26; John Seely Brown, Allan Collins, and Paul Duguid, "Situated Cognition and the Culture of Learning," *Educational Researcher* 18, no. 1 (1989): 32–42; Rogoff et al., "Development Through Participation"; Roland G. Tharp and Ronald Gallimore, *Rousing Minds to Life: Teaching, Learning, and Schooling in Social Context* (Cambridge: Cambridge University Press, 1991).

8. Albert Bandura, "Exercise of Human Agency Through Collective Efficacy," *Current Directions in Psychological Science* 9, no. 3 (2000): 75–78; Bransford, Brown, and Cocking, *How People Learn*.

9. Brown, Collins, and Duguid, "Situated Cognition"; Ann L. Brown and Joseph C. Campione, *Guided Discovery in a Community of Learners* (Cambridge, MA: MIT Press, 1994); Collins, Brown, and Holum, "Cognitive Apprenticeship"; Ilana Seidel Horn and Judith Warren Little, "Attending to Problems of Practice: Routines and Resources for Professional Learning in Teachers' Workplace Interactions," *American Educational Research Journal* 47, no. 1 (2010): 181–217; Jean Lave, "Teaching, as Learning, in Practice," *Mind, Culture, and Activity* 3, no. 3 (1996): 149–164; Jean Lave and Etienne Wenger, *Situated Learning: Legitimate Peripheral Participation* (Cambridge: Cambridge University Press, 1991); Smagorinsky, Cook, and Johnson, "The Twisting Path"; Tharp and Gallimore, *Rousing Minds to Life*; Wenger, *Communities of Practice*.

10. Honig and Rainey, *Supervising Principals for Instructional Leadership*.

Chapter 5

1. Other units traditionally called operational in our study districts included Human Resources, which we discuss in chapter 2, and also business services, which managed budgeting. Only one of our study districts engaged in transformation of business services. We address that limitation in chapter 7.

2. See, for example, Noel M. Tichy, *The Cycle of Leadership: How Great Leaders Teach Their Companies to Win*, Vol. 13 (New York: HarperCollins, 2002).

3. Yrjö Engeström, "From Design Experiments to Formative Interventions," *Theory & Psychology* 21, no. 5 (2011): 598–628; Samuel Severance et al., "Organizing for Teacher Agency in Curricular Co-Design," *Journal of the Learning Sciences* 25, no. 4 (2016): 531–564; Jaakko Virkkunen, "Dilemmas in Building Shared Transformative Agency," *Activités* 3, no. 3–1

(2006); Yrjö Engeström et al., "Grand Challenges for Future HCI Research: Cultures of Participation, Interfaces Supporting Learning, and Expansive Learning," in *Proceedings of the 6th Nordic Conference on Human-Computer Interaction: Extending Boundaries*, ed. Ebba Pora Hvannberg (New York: Association for Computing Machinery, 2010), 863–866; Arja Haapasaari, Yrjö Engeström, and Hannele Kerosuo, "The Emergence of Learners' Transformative Agency in a Change Laboratory Intervention," *Journal of Education and Work* 29, no. 2 (2016): 232–262; Arja Haapasaari and Hannele Kerosuo, "Transformative Agency: The Challenges of Sustainability in a Long Chain of Double Stimulation," *Learning, Culture and Social Interaction* 4 (2015): 37–47; Andreas Lund and Jon Magne Vestøl, "An Analytical Unit of Transformative Agency: Dynamics and Dialectics," *Learning, Culture and Social Interaction* 25 (2020): 2210–6561.

Chapter 6

1. Chris Argyris and Donald A. Schon, *Organizational Learning II: Theory, Method, Practice* (Boston: Addison-Wesley, 1996).
2. Brian Gil, Brandon Coffee Borden, and Kristin Hallgren, *A Conceptual Framework for Data-Driven Decision Making* (Princeton, NJ: Mathematica, 2014).
3. Michael A. Copland, "Leadership of Inquiry: Building and Sustaining Capacity for School Improvement," *Educational Evaluation and Policy Analysis* 25, no. 4 (2003): 375–395; Alicia C. Dowd and Roman Liera, "Sustaining Change Towards Racial Equity Through Cycles of Inquiry," *Education Policy Analysis Archives* 26, no. 6 (2018): 1–46.
4. Meredith I. Honig and Lydia R. Rainey, *Supervising Principals for Instructional Leadership: A Teaching and Learning Approach* (Cambridge, MA: Harvard Education Press, 2020).
5. Yrjö Engeström and Annalisa Sannino, "Studies of Expansive Learning: Foundations, Findings and Further Challenges," *Educational Research Review* 5 (2010): 1–24; Kris Gutiérrez, Yrjo Engeström, and Annalisa Sannino, "Expanding Educational Research and Interventionist Methodologies," *Cognition and Instruction* 34, no. 3 (2016): 275–284; Kris D. Gutiérrez and A. Susan Jurow, "Social Design Experiments: Toward Equity by Design," *Journal of the Learning Sciences* 25, no. 4 (2016): 565–598; Arja Haapasaari, Yrjö Engeström, and Hannele Kerosuo, "The Emergence of Learners' Transformative Agency in a Change Laboratory Intervention," *Journal of Education and Work* 29, no. 2 (2016): 232–262; Andreas Lund and Jon Magne Vestøl, "An Analytical Unit of Transformative Agency: Dynamics and Dialectics," *Learning, Culture and Social Interaction* 25 (2020): 1–9; Noel Tichy and Nancy Cardwell, *The Cycle of Leadership: How Great Leaders Teach Their Companies to Win* (New York: Harper Business, 2002).

6. Meredith I. Honig, Nitya Venkateswaran, and Patricia McNeil, "Research Use as Learning: The Case of Fundamental Change in School District Central Offices," *American Educational Research Journal* 54, no. 5 (2017): 938–971; Honig and Rainey, *Supervising Principals for Instructional Leadership.*

7. Noel Tichy, *Managing Strategic Change* (New York: Wiley, 1983); Tichy and Cardwell, *The Cycle of Leadership.*

8. Jean Lave and Etienne Wenger, *Situated Learning: Legitimate Peripheral Participation* (Cambridge: Cambridge University Press, 1991); Etienne Wenger, *Communities of Practice: Learning, Meaning, and Identity* (Cambridge: Cambridge University Press, 1999).

9. Sanne F. Akkerman and Arthur Bakker, "Boundary Crossing and Boundary Objects," *Review of Educational Research* 81, no. 2 (2011): 132–169; John Seely Brown and Paul Duguid, "Organizational Learning and Communities-of-Practice: Toward a Unified View of Working, Learning, and Innovation," *Organization Science* 2, no. 1 (1991): 40–57; Lave and Wenger, *Situated Learning*; Wenger, *Communities of Practice.*

10. Deborah G. Ancona and David F. Caldwell, "Bridging the Boundary: External Activity and Performance in Organizational Teams," *Administrative Science Quarterly* 37, no. 4 (1992): 634–665; Richard L. Daft and Karl E. Weick, "Toward a Model of Organizations as Interpretation Systems," *Academy of Management Review* 9, no. 2 (1984): 284–295.

11. As we discuss further in chapter 7, the central office transformation efforts in most districts were cost neutral or cost savings because they required the redirection of core resources.

About the Authors

Meredith I. Honig is professor of Education Policy, Organizations, and Leadership and director of the District Leadership Design Lab (DL2, dl2.education.uw.edu) at the University of Washington, where she also is an adjunct professor of Public Affairs. Her current research and partnerships focus on the redesign of school district central offices to ensure that all students experience an excellent and equitable education, especially students identifying as Black, Indigenous, and Latinx; students of color; and students living in low-income circumstances. Her work recognizes that barriers to educational equity are systemic, that school district central office leaders are in strategic positions to ensure educational equity, and that those leaders would benefit from new knowledge and support for their leadership.

Honig has published widely in academic and practitioner-focused journals and other outlets. Her books include *Supervising Principals for Instructional Leadership* (with Lydia R. Rainey, Cambridge, MA: Harvard Education Press, 2020).

In 2014, Honig and Rainey established DL2 to help district leaders access knowledge and tools to transform their central offices into engines of educational equity. Between 2012 and 2018, she directed the Leadership for Learning (EdD) program, which won the Exemplary Educational Leadership Program award from the University Council for Educational Administration in 2016. Honig received her BA from Brown University and her PhD from Stanford University.

Lydia R. Rainey is a research scientist at the Mary Lou Fulton Teachers College at Arizona State University and a principal at the Center on Reinventing Public Education (CRPE). Since 2000, Rainey has researched ways to design and implement equitable and innovative school systems, with attention to how our current systems often preserve the status quo. Her recent research has focused on how educational leaders in state agencies, central offices, and schools lead the design and implementation of new policies and practices that call for deep changes in how their school system educates students. She approaches this work using traditional qualitative, quantitative, and design-based techniques.

Prior to joining CRPE, Rainey worked with Honig at DL2 as well as at the University of Washington's Center for Teaching and Policy and the City of Seattle Office of Education. Rainey has a PhD in Education Policy, Organizations, and Leadership; an MPA; and a BA in Political Economy, all from the University of Washington.

Index